Selling Social Justice

The Jacobin series features short interrogations of politics, economics, and culture from a socialist perspective, as an avenue to radical political practice. The books offer critical analysis and engagement with the history and ideas of the Left in an accessible format.

The series is a collaboration between Verso Books and *Jacobin* magazine, which is published quarterly in print and online at jacobinmag.com.

Other titles in this series from Verso Books include:

Selling Social Justice

Why the Rich Love Antiracism

JENNIFER C. PAN

VERSO

London • New York

For my parents and Angela, who first told me to write it down

First published by Verso 2025
© Jennifer C. Pan 2025

1 3 5 7 9 10 8 6 4 2

Verso
UK: 6 Meard Street, London W1F 0EG
US: 207 East 32nd Street, New York, NY 10016
versobooks.com

Verso is the imprint of New Left Books

ISBN-13: 978-1-80429-422-2
ISBN-13: 978-1-80429-423-9 (UK EBK)
ISBN-13: 978-1-80429-424-6 (US EBK)

British Library Cataloguing in Publication Data
A catalogue record for this book is available from the British Library

Library of Congress Cataloging-in-Publication Data

Names: Pan, Jennifer C., author.
Title: Selling social justice : why the rich love antiracism / Jennifer C.
    Pan.
Description: London ; New York : Verso, 2025. | Series: Jacobin | Includes
    bibliographical references.
Identifiers: LCCN 2024051340 (print) | LCCN 2024051341 (ebook) | ISBN
    9781804294222 (trade paperback) | ISBN 9781804294246 (ebook)
Subjects: LCSH: Social justice. | Anti-racism. | Rich people—Attitudes.
Classification: LCC HM671 .P358 2025 (print) | LCC HM671 (ebook) | DDC
    305.8—dc23/eng/20241226
LC record available at https://lccn.loc.gov/2024051340
LC ebook record available at https://lccn.loc.gov/2024051341

Typeset in Fournier MT by Hewer Text UK Ltd, Edinburgh
Printed and bound by CPI Group (UK) Ltd, Croydon CR0 4YY

CONTENTS

INTRODUCTION

One year, after several incidents of racial violence too gruesome even for white Americans to ignore, the nation experienced a profound crisis of consciousness over its long legacy
of racism. Essays on the poisonous reach of white supremacy
filled publications like the *Nation* and the *New Republic*; activists launched a flurry of new organizations and initiatives
dedicated to fighting racial injustice. That year at its national
convention, the Democratic Party enshrined its commitment
to antiracism in its official platform. The issue was so pressing,
the historian Peter J. Kellogg observed, that even in a bitterly
divided Congress, "there seemed to be a wide, if far from
universal, consensus that something should be done about
racism."[1] It was 1948.

Every society-wide racial reckoning, so to speak, arises from
its particular political and economic moment. At the end of the
1940s, as support for civil rights was beginning to build on a
national scale, the United States had just concluded fighting in
World War II and both political parties were competing fiercely
for black voters in a closely watched presidential election. The

public reckoning on race that ensued that decade was partly a matter of political pragmatism: At their convention, the Democrats adopted an official civil rights plank for the first time in a bid to attract a decisive share of black voters. And for the liberal intelligentsia of that era, Kellogg writes, the racial reckoning also presented an opportunity to resolve a serious moral conundrum. American liberals had been increasingly horrified by the similarities they observed between the Nazi atrocities in Europe and lynchings of blacks in the supposedly advanced US. Against the backdrop of World War II, the racial reckoning of the 1940s was at once an interparty contest for political dominance and a means to rehabilitate the concept of American democracy.

Nearly eighty years later, another national reckoning on race would commence a different kind of rehabilitative project.

The nationwide protests against police violence and racial inequality that exploded following the police murder of George Floyd in Minneapolis on Memorial Day of 2020 inaugurated a uniquely twenty-first-century racial reckoning. Though Floyd's death was by no means the first police killing of an unarmed black man captured on video, nor the first to spark widespread protests, that summer, a record number of people in the US—between 15 to 26 million, according to the *New York Times*—participated in racial justice demonstrations.[2] Public support for Black Lives Matter reached an all-time high, and politicians across the political spectrum, including notoriously law-and-order-inclined Republicans, vehemently condemned racism and the Minneapolis officers' brutality. "Americans from coast to coast have been grieved and horrified by the killings of African American citizens: Ahmaud Arbery in Georgia, Breonna Taylor in my hometown of Louisville, Kentucky, and George Floyd in Minneapolis," Senator Mitch McConnell said in a statement a few days after Floyd's death. "Our nation cannot deafen itself to the anger, pain, or frustration of black Americans."[3] For left-wing activists, the size and scale of the protests that engulfed the streets that summer suggested that the moment was the long-awaited catalyst of a society-wide transformative movement from below—the very movement that Occupy Wall Street and two Bernie Sanders campaigns had ultimately failed to ignite. "It's official, the Movement for Black Lives is now the largest protest movement in US history!" the progressive advocacy group Working Families Party declared in a July fundraising dispatch. "People have been showing up for Black lives by the millions and it is already changing America."[4]

In a sense the group was right: The protests of 2020 and their aftermath would come to represent an inflection point in an ongoing transformation of the country. It wasn't, however, America's working families or even most black Americans who stood to gain from the moment, urgent and righteous as it seemed that summer. Instead, it was the ruling class that would emerge not only as a major sponsor of the racial reckoning but also as its primary beneficiary.

That year the richest and most powerful institutions and individuals in the US eagerly underwrote the demand for racial justice. According to an estimate by the consulting firm McKinsey, corporations and the financial sector together poured a staggering $340 billion into racial equity measures in the

wake of Floyd's death, ranging from grants for black entrepreneurs to investments in affordable housing.[5] Between 2020
and 2021, the philanthropic sector funded racial justice initiatives to the tune of $23 billion—or approximately $20 billion
more than they had spent on such projects over the prior nine
years combined—with the Ford Foundation alone pledging $3
billion.[6] Individual funders, too, rose to the occasion: Finance
heiress Susan Sandler donated $200 million to racial justice
organizations while philanthropist Mackenzie Scott, fresh from
a lucrative divorce from Amazon's Jeff Bezos, committed
nearly $587 million. "Like many, I watched the first half of
2020 with a mixture of heartbreak and horror," Scott wrote in
a statement. "People troubled by recent events can make new
connections between privileges they've enjoyed and benefits
they've taken for granted."[7]

What had compelled the rich to embrace antiracism with such
fervor? No doubt many, like the demonstrators who flooded
the streets that summer, were horrified by the brutal killings of
George Floyd and other black Americans. But the ruling-class
enthusiasm for antiracism in 2020 also served a broader purpose.
If the racial reckoning of 1948 had occurred during a period of
relative prosperity and a lingering sense of wartime unity, the
twenty-first-century version had unfolded not only at a time
of extreme and worsening economic inequality but also amid
a profound economic crack-up that the rich were anxious to
resolve. As author Nicole Aschoff has noted, "Capital's ability
to periodically present a new set of legitimating principles that
facilitate the willing participation of society accounts for its
remarkable longevity despite periodic bouts of deep crisis."[8]

This book tells the story of how contemporary antiracism—understood as the commitment to eliminating racial disparities from all areas of American life—became a means for the rich to re-legitimize a floundering capitalist order in the twenty-first century.

For most of America's past, it was racism—that is, the belief that distinct races exist and that some are superior to others—that had functioned as a practical and effective tool for economic and political elites to entrench their position at the top of a socioeconomic hierarchy. The myth of black racial inferiority, for instance, had served as an ideological justification for the use of slave labor in the antebellum South and then as a means for the planter class to reassert its dominance by disenfranchising newly emancipated blacks after Reconstruction. Employers throughout the better part of the next century likewise stoked racial prejudice to undercut or preempt working-class alliances by, for example, crafting ornate eugenicist taxonomies to sort workers of different ethnicities into different occupations or dangling the promise of jobs before unemployed blacks in order to use them as strikebreakers during labor disputes with unionized white workforces.

This history is now so shameful—and the civil rights movement that emerged to challenge racial inequality so venerated—that it has tended to overshadow another type of affinity that the rich have held for race. While plenty of reactionaries throughout the twentieth century continued to find ways to wield racist ideas and discriminatory practices to consolidate their wealth and power, by the end of World War II, overt white supremacy, Kellogg notes, "was no longer a publicly acceptable doctrine in the North." Over the next decades, an increasing number of economic and political elites would distinguish themselves by promoting *antiracism*. In 1964, the same year that segregationist George Wallace ran for president, the mayor of Atlanta and the CEO of Coca-Cola hosted an integrated dinner honoring Martin Luther King Jr. and used their combined influence to persuade conservative white business leaders in the city to attend the event. By the end of the '60s, the Ford Foundation had begun awarding its largest grants to civil rights groups like the NAACP and the National Urban League.

Shrewd politicians soon found more ways to invoke antiracism to their advantage. Though Richard Nixon had notoriously campaigned on the so-called Southern strategy—deploying coded, racially charged appeals to attract white Southern voters to the Republican Party—once in office, he threw his support behind affirmative action. In 1969, his administration initiated the Philadelphia Plan, an unprecedented program requiring federal contractors to hire black workers according to strict timelines. As historian Judith Stein has written, Nixon's primary concern was driving down inflation, which his administration attributed to rising construction costs.[9] They viewed forcing the integration of the predominantly white construction industry as a means of expanding the labor pool and pushing down high construction wages while simultaneously undermining the powerful building trades unions. The president, Stein writes, also "appreciated the possibilities of dividing civil rights groups and labor" at a time when the economy was in flux and employment was down, thereby fracturing the Democratic base.

But if Nixon's support for affirmative action had been mostly a matter of political expedience, today the ruling-class penchant for antiracism has expanded into an aggressive ideological campaign to mystify and maintain the present economic order. The winners of the current regime—big business, wealthy philanthropists, and affluent professionals, among others—have advocated antiracism in total earnestness because the type of reorganization of society that such an ideology entails ultimately poses very little threat to their power or status. Contemporary capitalism, to put it another way, can happily accommodate and even endorse antiracism while also necessitating the continued exploitation of the vast majority of people on earth.

This is why, in 2020, corporate America immediately threw its considerable weight behind the pursuit of racial equity. These efforts were not, as some have suggested, merely a cynical "co-optation" of the protests but rather part of a much larger effort on the part of big business to secure its continued political dominance and circumvent government regulation. Likewise, employers that summer rushed to adopt a battery of diversity, equity, and inclusion measures not only as window dressing but more fundamentally as a way of surveilling and disciplining their workforces while also staving off union organizing. Meanwhile, Democratic Party leaders and liberal professionals in white-collar and creative fields doubled down on the notion of race as the country's most significant and enduring dividing line and pushed a host of controversial ideas and regressive policies under the guise of ameliorating disparities, with the effect of displacing the question of class and exacerbating a decades-long working-class exodus from the party. And the right responded to the outpouring by launching its own sustained broadside against "wokeness" and "critical race theory," fueling a highly charged partisan culture war that has served only as a toxic distraction from the continued economic pressure on all workers.

Today it's not particularly difficult to understand the moral appeal of antiracism, which remains, at its very best, a belief system that asserts the full humanity and inherent worth of every person regardless of the racial identity ascribed to them and soundly rejects notions of biological racial difference that have been used to justify violence against certain groups or otherwise consign these groups to second-class citizenship. But the righteousness of the cause in the abstract has clouded the fact that, in practice, antiracism in the twenty-first century increasingly serves to stabilize the economic status quo and obfuscate class inequality, which is, ironically, not unlike the work that racism performed a century earlier. Despite its promise to conjure a more egalitarian world, antiracism has instead come to be a powerful legitimating ideology of a deeply unequal economic order.

1

THE ROAD TO RECKONING

"Black Lives Matter. And so do Black voices," went one representative corporate statement released in June of 2020. "We are devastated by the murders of George Floyd, Breonna Taylor, Ahmaud Arbery, and countless others who have been killed. We stand with those fighting for justice."

That was the official pronouncement on the importance of racial justice from the fruit snack brand Gushers, which added, "Gushers wouldn't be Gushers without the Black community and your voices."[1] As protests continued across the country that summer, they were accompanied by an avalanche of support from corporate America. Businesses that had never previously expressed much interest in rectifying social inequality—and even those with well-documented histories of labor abuses, questionable campaign contributions, and racial discrimination—were newly eager to demonstrate their antiracism. "If you tolerate racism, *delete Uber*," instructed one billboard rushed out by the notoriously exploitative rideshare company that summer.[2]

And if corporations' statements on race and racism in America had once been limited to platitudes celebrating "diversity" and "differences," in 2020, the canniest executives realized that it would cost them nothing to trade the stale language of '90s multiculturalism for more radical, movement-style rhetoric. Condemnations of "systemic racism" or "structural racism"—once the near-exclusive vocabulary of academics and activists—became standard talking points in the corporate PR flood that year. A few days after Floyd's death, Google CEO Sundar Pichai wrote in a company memo, "Violent and racist attacks against the Black community have forced the world to reckon with the structural and systemic racism that Black people have experienced over generations. Systemic racism permeates every aspect of life, from interactions with law enforcement, to access to housing and capital, to health care, education, and the workplace."[3] Not to be outdone, Amazon's official statement on the protests read, "The inequitable and brutal treatment of Black people in our country must stop. Together we stand in solidarity with the Black community—our employees, customers, and partners—in the fight against systemic racism and injustice."[4]

For some, this outpouring was a welcome sign of progress. Kimberlé Crenshaw, the legal scholar who coined the term "intersectionality," argued that the newly militant rhetoric from the private sector outshone even that of the left-wing senator Bernie Sanders. "You basically have a moment where every corporation worth its salt is saying something about structural racism and anti-blackness, and that stuff is even outdistancing what candidates in the Democratic Party were actually saying," she told the *New York Times*.[5] Other commentators, suspicious of the business sector's sudden passion for racial justice, demanded to see more than statements. "A lot of times you look at what companies are saying, and then you look at what candidates and issues they're supporting, and there's a deep incongruence there, if not hypocrisy," journalist Nikole Hannah-Jones said on a *Times* podcast. In her view, she added, corporate America had a "much, much larger role to play" in fighting racial inequity.[6]

Corporations appeared to agree. That year, big business also opened its coffers to the cause. In the fall, the Business Roundtable—the most powerful and well-organized capitalist lobby in America—convened a special meeting to announce the rollout of a number of initiatives "to advance racial equity and justice," including a pledge of $900 million in funding from the Roundtable for HBCUs and a commitment to using the political might of the organization to press Congress for policing reform.[7] More than a hundred Roundtable members made additional individual donations: Walmart, Apple, and Comcast all committed at least $100 million each to racial equity initiatives; Chase alone pledged a staggering $30 billion for programs to close the racial wealth gap.[8] By the end of just that year, McKinsey estimated that corporate America had collectively given more than $200 billion to racial justice.

This avalanche of donations was, of course, partially a public relations maneuver. Even prior to the pandemic, Americans had been souring on the notion of unchecked corporate power; polling in the years leading up to 2020 indicated that public opinion on corporations was dismal. According to Gallup, around 60 percent of Americans had consistently expressed dissatisfaction with the size and influence of major corporations in the US almost every year between 2010 and 2020.[9] Likewise, in a 2017 survey of 10,000 people, two-thirds said they distrusted the Fortune 500, with 85 percent of Democrats—and a somewhat surprising 72 percent of Republicans—agreeing that companies shared too little of their success with employees.[10] In 2020, at the height of the catastrophic Covid-19 pandemic in which corporate profits rose unhindered just as the public was reeling from mass layoffs, inflation, and soaring Covid death rates, the protests offered an opening for a business sector fattened by decades of deregulation, tax cuts, and stock buybacks to launder its tarnished image.

But ostentatious as it was, the enthusiasm for racial justice charities and new diversity initiatives from the business sector in 2020 wasn't only moral grandstanding or a bid for positive press. The corporate support for racial justice that year was rather part of a larger capitalist attempt to shock new life into the economic order precisely at a moment when public trust in that order—and the stability of the system itself—was rapidly disintegrating.

The Insidious Allure of Progressive Neoliberalism

A century earlier, elites had reliably leveraged racism to their benefit by encouraging and inflaming divisions between workers and citizens of different races. Racial animus, as W. E. B. Du Bois famously wrote in *Black Reconstruction*, was "a carefully planned and slowly evolved method" designed not only to physically and socially separate black and white workers from one another but also to conceal the fact that these two groups in reality held "practically identical interests." From the end of the nineteenth century to the middle of the twentieth, reactionary politicians and an emboldened capitalist class had ruthlessly enforced the segregationist Jim Crow order and violently subordinated blacks—not simply because they considered them inferior to whites, but more practically to secure their continued economic and political dominance by crushing an emergent cross-racial populist movement of farmers and sharecroppers.

Though codified racial hierarchy had certainly helped buoy capitalist power for the first half of the twentieth century, this divide-and-conquer function of racism evolved in several notable ways following the high period of the civil rights movement. Civil rights activism hadn't wholly eliminated racism from American life, but by the end of the 1960s it had nevertheless succeeded in re-enfranchising Southern blacks, ending de jure segregation, and outlawing discrimination in employment, housing, and other areas. Over the next decades, the formal integration of schools and workplaces also dramatically eroded racial prejudice and biases among individuals; for instance, while just 4 percent of the public in 1948 said they approved of interracial marriage between blacks and whites, by 2021 that approval rate had increased to a nearly unanimous 94 percent.[11] And by the close of the century, the consolidation of a new economic order quickly gave rise to a political consensus that proved surprisingly accommodating of the idea of racial diversity even as it simultaneously turbocharged economic inequality and drove an ever-increasing number of working people toward financial insecurity.

Neoliberalism, the economic regime that has governed American life from the end of the 1970s to the present day, was embraced by policymakers as a scheme to jumpstart a slowing postwar economy. Neoliberal fiscal policy was orga-nized broadly around massive tax cuts for businesses and the wealthy, aggressive deregulation of the financial sector, the privatization (or elimination) of public goods, and a methodical smashing of organized labor. According to its evangelists, once businesses were relieved of high tax burdens and combative unions, they would in turn use the resulting boost in their profits to stimulate economic growth by creating new jobs, raising wages, and buying or producing the necessary goods, equipment, and technology to increase labor productivity. Over the next decades, the private sector collectively embraced the so-called Friedman Doctrine, the 1970 free market urtext that asserted that a corporation's sole responsibility was to increase its profits and deliver its shareholders as much money as possible. This ruthless strategy, combined with generous government subsidies and the rollback of labor laws, would send corporate profits soaring.

But if neoliberalism represented the triumph of capital over labor, it was also a system that would come to accommodate—even welcome—elements of social radicalism. Neoliberalism's ideological architects, the historian Gary Gerstle has noted, "saw in market freedom an opportunity to fashion a self or iden-tity that was free of tradition, inheritance, and prescribed social roles."[12] This spirit of antiauthoritarianism and individualism gave rise to a strain of capitalism far less culturally conserva-tive than its predecessor. The opposition to formal hierarchy, social conformity, and state control that characterized the free market ethos was also shared by many of the social movements of the 1960s, producing a strange kind of symbiosis between the new economic regime and the anti-oppression politics of the postwar period. As Gerstle has argued, neoliberalism "drew energy from the liberation movements originating in the New Left—black power, feminism, multiculturalism, and gay pride among them."[13] In turn, the incorporation of those progressive elements into the neoliberal order would come to legitimize the system for a great many people living under it.

The bipartisan enthusiasm for neoliberalism that took shape over the next forty years was made possible, at least in part, by this dynamism. While the Republican Party from Ronald Reagan onward formed its electoral base by courting social conservatives and economic libertarians alike, Democratic elites increasingly oriented their party around what the political theorist Nancy Fraser has called "progressive neoliberalism"—that is, an entanglement of free market economics and progressive cultural values like cosmopolitanism, gender equality, antiracism, and sexual freedom.[14] Today's avatars of this sort of politics include California governor Gavin Newsom, a former business mogul turned politician who launched himself to liberal stardom in 2004 when, as the newly elected mayor of San Francisco, he issued marriage licenses to same-sex couples in the city in defiance of what was then state law. During his tenure as governor, Newsom has continued to burnish his credentials as a blue-state culture warrior through championing various gender and racial equity initiatives, including mandating ethnic studies courses in public schools and instituting board diversity requirements for all corporations headquartered in California. But behind this progressive pageantry is the fact that California remains one of the most unaffordable and economically unequal states in the country and, in recent years, has held the highest poverty rate of any state in the union.[15]

The end vision of progressive neoliberalism is, in the words of sociologist Dylan Riley, "a profoundly unequal but rigorously equitable form of capitalism," or a society that's no less economically stratified than it is now but also one that doesn't preemptively constrain people by their race (or gender or sexuality) from rising to the top (or sinking to the bottom).[16] What continues to give this impoverished framework of justice its progressive gloss is that there's a wing of the Republican Party that still trades in overt racism and nativism. But a choice between market fundamentalism yoked to racial resentment and market fundamentalism yoked to racial equity is a rather miserable one indeed. And yet it's the only choice that the two major political parties in the US have offered citizens for decades.

The Neoliberal Order in Crisis

Today it's difficult to deny that the enormous wealth generated by four decades of corporate tax breaks and relentless union busting never quite trickled down as promised. Though wide-scale neoliberal restructuring did deliver a windfall to the business sector, corporations began funneling those profits to offshore accounts, shareholder dividends and stock buybacks, and exorbitant CEO compensation packages in lieu of investing capital in production and jobs. Meanwhile, policymakers at every level of government entrenched free market worship across party lines. American neoliberalism had been catalyzed by Ronald Reagan, but it was Bill Clinton's Democratic administration that completed the project in the 1990s through the deregulation of Wall Street, the championing of punitive austerity policies like welfare reform, and the passage of NAFTA, a free trade agreement that kneecapped the domestic manufacturing sector and, by extension, much of the American working class.

The cumulative effect of nearly half a century of declining worker power and ruling-class hoarding has been a dramatic widening of the distance between the haves and have-nots. Since the end of the 1970s, income and wealth inequality in the US have expanded to Gilded Age levels; as the economist Thomas Piketty has observed, the lion's share of economic gains over this time have gone straight to the top 1 percent of income earners, leaving everyone else to divide the crumbs. By contrast, the average worker's wages since the '70s have stagnated even as productivity has consistently risen, and executive compensation has soared to nauseating heights. The end result of this decades-long fiscal policy has been what amounts to a massive upward transfer of wealth from working people to the rich; one analysis by the RAND Corporation estimated that so-called trickle-down economics had in fact succeeded in redistributing $50 trillion from the bottom 90 percent of Americans to the top 1 percent between 1975 and 2018.[17]

The brutality of this economic status quo became explicit following the disastrous 2008 recession in which the very banks that caused the crash were bailed out while workers were left to fend for themselves in a wave of job layoffs and home foreclosures. The legitimacy of the neoliberal order cratered during the recession's putative recovery period, which continued to deliver over 85 percent of all new income growth to the top 1 percent while the majority of workers' wages remained flat.[18] In addition to its reputational crisis, neoliberalism also appeared to be approaching a structural predicament in the wake of the crash as economic growth stalled and consumer and private-sector debt snowballed, despite a regular government supply of tax cuts and corporate subsidies intended to promote new growth.

Neoliberalism has since idled in this state of slow-motion decay. The economic and political malaise generated by runaway income and wealth inequality and a recession that was left to fester would allow insurgent presidential candidates Bernie Sanders and Donald Trump to upend American politics in one short campaign cycle in 2016. The unexpected success of both politicians—the former a self-described democratic socialist advocating a New Deal–style expansion of public goods and the latter a brash businessman hawking right-wing nationalism with a dash of protectionist rhetoric—represented two poles of unhappiness with America's floundering economic order. Though Trump's upset victory in the election over Hillary Clinton was less the result of a popular mandate than it was the consequence of an antidemocratic electoral college system, Clinton's crushing losses in the Rust Belt—a former labor and Democratic stronghold—nevertheless suggested a deep disillusionment among voters with a Democratic Party entranced by free market dogma and openly eager to swap its working-class constituents for Wall Street donors.

Such conditions were only compounded by the chaotic

Trump presidency. Before the end of Trump's term, the economy buckled again as a once-in-a-generation pandemic sent markets tumbling and ground businesses and global supply chains to halt. Covid-19 threw into sharp relief the deep dysfunction of the economic regime just a little over a decade after the Great Recession had already delivered a crippling blow to its legitimacy and stability. That spring, as Covid hospitalizations and deaths spiked and millions found themselves out of jobs in the wake of widespread business shutdowns, the federal government scrambled to assemble a makeshift social safety net after decades of deliberately razing the one that had been forged during the New Deal. Though Congress eventually passed a Covid relief package that secured expanded unemployment benefits and stimulus checks for Americans, it was only after a bitter political battle in which Republicans fought tooth and nail to strip down the bill's provisions or attach punitive work requirements to them.

The economic shock of the pandemic and the inability or unwillingness of the government to stanch the subsequent hardship beyond a handful of stopgap measures exacerbated the already yawning chasm between the rich and the poor. Workers around the world lost an estimated $3.7 trillion in earnings, and lines gathered at food banks as families' emergency funds dwindled.[19] According to one report, almost a fifth of US households had drained their entire savings by the following year.[20] The social isolation imposed by the lockdowns was accompanied by alarming increases in rates of mental illness, gun violence, and drug overdoses, primarily among the working class and the poor. The wealthiest Americans, on the other hand, emerged from the disaster not only financially unscathed, but somehow even richer. Billionaires reaped a combined $5 trillion during the pandemic thanks to the wild fluctuations of the stock market, and profits at the very same companies whose essential workforces had been hit hardest by the virus soared.[21] (Bernie Sanders, for his part, called on Congress to levy a one-time tax on this obscene amount of corporate and individual wealth, to no avail.)

By the middle of 2020, acute (if largely disorganized) dissatisfaction with the neoliberal order had bubbled over in several ways. The protests that erupted that summer were partly spurred by a buildup of frustration over months of Covid lockdowns and anxiety surrounding the pandemic and the Trump administration's haphazard response to it. Like other Black Lives Matter actions that had come before, they were also an impassioned reaction to the indignity and violence of what the political scientist Cedric Johnson has called stress policing, or the style of law enforcement that emerged out of the carceral expansion of the 1980s. Stress policing, which functions in large part to transform formerly disinvested city centers into areas palatable to real estate interests and upscale residents, primarily targets the unemployed and the most dispossessed, who, in urban areas, tend disproportionately to be black. As Johnson has written, "Black Lives Matter emerged amid the worsening conditions created by neoliberal rollback, which hit specific layers of the black population especially hard."[22]

The 2020 demonstrations, in other words, did constitute a genuine revolt against the status quo. Yet, the cultural reckoning that bloomed, earnest as it may have been, never posed any kind of threat to the ruling class. Instead, it offered an occasion for elites to redouble their efforts to rehabilitate the economic system that had delivered them their riches and political power in the first place. Though fissures in the order have steadily widened and popular dissatisfaction with the punishing trickle-down consensus has mounted, there are few signs that a more egalitarian economy is currently in the making. The winners of the neoliberal regime furthermore have every incentive to keep it on life support for as long as possible. As Gerstle put it, "There will be structures—ideological and institutional—that survive and prolong the life of neoliberalism in some form."[23]

The Ascendance of Stakeholder Capitalism

While the George Floyd protests had unleashed an unprecedented flood of social justice commitments from the corporate sector, nearly a year earlier, the Business Roundtable had already openly committed to a kinder, more socially conscious approach to making money. In a public statement released in 2019, nearly 200 of the country's leading CEOs proclaimed that they would no longer run their corporations solely for the enrichment of shareholders.[24] Instead, they promised, they would conduct business in a manner that considered the well-being of all *stakeholders*, including suppliers, customers, employees, and even the general public. This new way of doing business, advocates insisted, would prioritize values neglected by the principles of the Friedman Doctrine, including environmental sustainability and racial equity. "Major employers are investing in their workers and communities because they know it is the only way to be successful over the long term," JP Morgan Chase CEO Jamie Dimon said. "These modernized principles reflect the business community's unwavering commitment to continue to push for an economy that serves all Americans."[25]

Dozens of other private sector titans had exactly the same inclination. At the start of the next year, the World Economic Forum (WEF)—the lobbying organization that sponsors the annual Davos conference that convenes some of the richest and most powerful people in world—crafted a new manifesto that laid out a twenty-first-century blueprint for stakeholder capitalism. Running companies with an eye for environmental and social justice, WEF founder Klaus Schwab wrote, would not only ensure the longevity of capitalism but would also position "private corporations as trustees of society."[26] A few months later, the consulting giant McKinsey, which has advised nearly every Fortune 500 company at one point or another, also publicly affirmed its commitment to the stakeholder model. "We want to leave the world a better place; we want to lead responsibly," senior partner Vivian Hunt said in a statement. "Stakeholder capitalism is a framework to do so."[27]

What had prompted a capitalist class at the apex of its wealth and political power to endorse the concept of stakeholder capitalism after decades of unflagging adherence to the Friedman Doctrine? The feel-good explanation for corporate America's growing concern over problems like climate change and racial injustice is that it represents a response to public pressure, if not some kind of collective moral epiphany on the part of business leaders. ("I think woke capitalism represents a substantive victory of the left and the forces of justice," professor and progressive commentator Olúfẹ́mi O. Táíwò said in a 2020 magazine interview.)[28] But the truth is that stakeholder capitalism is less a straightforward instance of the public bending corporations toward enlightened attitudes than it is a calculated choice on the part of big business to shed some of the more punishing aspects of free market convictions in order to manage a crumbling economic regime and expand into select customer bases.

By the time the Business Roundtable had released its paean to stakeholder capitalism, it was clear to a growing number of business leaders and policymakers alike that the corporate obligation to maximize short-term shareholder returns at all costs was hastening economic and political instability around the globe. Forty years of shareholder primacy had generated what the *Harvard Business Review* dubbed "profits without prosperity"—that is, outrageous wealth for a small number of executives and shareholders at the expense of the larger economy.[29] Shareholder primacy was also beginning to undermine business growth itself by cannibalizing earnings that might have otherwise been reinvested in production or labor. "One of the main reasons why world growth has been subpar has been because businesses have not been investing sufficiently," Andy Haldane, the Bank of England's chief economist, told the BBC in 2015. "They're almost eating themselves. They're taking their internal funds and distributing that to shareholders rather than investing in themselves."[30]

In other words, while stakeholder capitalism might seem like a friendlier, more sustainable alternative to the shareholder mania of the golden age of neoliberalism, it represents

the latest attempt by the private sector to safeguard its own
interests, not any kind of sign of progress or victory for the
public. The stakeholder model is an expression of the business
sector's awareness that their own fortunes depend on finding
a way to blunt the mounting economic and political upheavals that they themselves have unleashed over time. And by its
advocates' own admission, the turn to stakeholder capitalism
isn't simply a matter of positive public relations; it's more
crucially about stabilizing and relegitimizing the economic
status quo. Ruling class institutions, the scholar Kyle Bailey
has noted, "have increasingly turned to 'stakeholder capitalism' as an ideological formation congruent with managing the
new 'systemic risks' thrown up by the intensifying crises of
neoliberalism."[31] Or, as the *Harvard Business Review* put it a
few months into the pandemic, "It's time we get serious about
writing a new chapter on capitalism, before it's too late."[32]

As I explore in more depth in chapter 4, a growing chorus
of right-wing opponents have decried the recent wave of
corporate activism as a neo-Marxist plot. However, stakeholder capitalism is, in fact, a consolidation of *business* power.
The very idea that the private sector could and should be an
engine of social change, after all, was made ubiquitous under
the fifty-year neoliberal era in which the US government
declined to guarantee necessities like health care or housing to its citizens, slow climate change, or eradicate poverty
and instead left those problems and others to be sorted out
by the market. The result of continuous privatization and
the destruction of the social safety net has been a vacuum
in which the business class is perfectly positioned to use its

power, money, and political influence to further undermine the public good, then turn around and offer stakeholder capitalism as a solution.

And, of course, no matter how enlightened corporations may seem these days, their political dominance and profit margins are inevitably still where the rubber meets the road, which means that for all of their recent progressive signaling, you'd be hard-pressed to find a corporation advocating for, say, expanded labor rights, campaign finance reform, or higher taxes. Plenty of companies that have proudly displayed their support for racial justice in the form of internal diversity, equity, and inclusion measures or large donations to charities have simultaneously engaged in tax evasion, union busting, and relentless political lobbying to roll back labor protections and other laws that threaten to cut into their profit or their influence on policymaking. Less than a year after condemning the "brutal treatment of black people" in the US, for instance, Amazon would crush a union drive at a Bessemer, Alabama, warehouse where more than 85 percent of the workers were black; likewise, executives at Bank of America, which had committed $1.25 billion to racial equity programs in 2020, later fretted in a memo that the tightening post-pandemic labor market appeared to be affording workers a little too much leverage.[33]

But the most insidious thing about stakeholder capitalism isn't that it enables corporate hypocrisy or PR stunts. The fundamental problem is rather that stakeholder capitalism further entrenches the strength of the private sector by allowing business to exert increased influence on national politics and to circumvent government regulation. Above all, stakeholder capitalism is an ideology that insists that big business can be trusted to usher in a more just society by promoting antiracism, safeguarding the environment, and improving the lives of workers, all without external pressure or oversight from the government or labor unions and certainly without sacrificing profit. This isn't exclusively cynical pandering: Some of the richest business moguls and the most devoted champions of stakeholder capitalism genuinely seem to believe big business can and should use their immense power and wealth for good. "Business is arguably the most powerful institution on the planet," business professor Rebecca Henderson wrote in 2021. "Only firms can drive the innovation we need at a scale that can solve today's environmental problems and generate the jobs upon which decent lives are built."[34]

The thought of the very same corporate sector that poured accelerant on the economic and social crises we now face undergoing a change of heart and riding to the rescue is a comforting story for those still attached to the promise of a free market. But no matter how powerful big business may be and no matter how guilty its more socially conscious leaders may now feel, in a capitalist economy, the survival of every firm—even those committed to prioritizing "stakeholders"—still depends on its ability to stay competitive. That all but ensures that sooner or later, the imperative to turn a profit will conflict with even the most earnest desire to do good. During the postwar period, concessions to workers and the general public were wrested from business by a powerful New Deal coalition and a fighting labor movement. But absent that kind of political force, today's stakeholder model offers only a hollow imitation of a compromise between big business and the public good.

This arrangement, of course, suits capitalists just fine. Behind the self-styled conscientiousness of stakeholder capitalism lies the potential for corporate America to retain and tighten its already ironclad grip on national politics. Though stakeholder capitalism may indeed spur some social change, that progress comes at the expense of the democratic process itself. The appeal of self-administered social responsibility for corporations is that it allows them to stave off government scrutiny and regulatory laws. There have already been at least a few brazen attempts by companies to invoke stakeholder capitalism to that end: At a 2022 Senate hearing on antitrust enforcement, for instance, Federal Trade Commission chair Lina Khan noted that she had encountered a number of corporations that had tried to brandish their various social responsibility initiatives—today most frequently shorthanded as "environmental, social, and corporate governance" measures, or ESG—to skirt antitrust regulation. "Firms come to us and say, 'We're proposing this merger that you'll probably identify as unlawful, but we'll make all of these ESG commitments, and you should take those as a reason to bless the merger," she said at the hearing. "We've seen firms come to us and try to claim an ESG exemption. We explain to them clearly that there is no such thing."[35]

This eagerness to dodge state oversight and public control also explains why large firms and their owners have been far more willing to donate significant sums of their wealth than have it taxed away. Taxation, at least in theory, returns decision-making to the public; charity allows rich benefactors to mold the political landscape to their tastes by funding the causes that they personally support. In 2020, for instance, Jeff Bezos pledged $10 billion to fight climate change in one of the largest known philanthropic donations ever made by an individual.[36] It was also approximately three times what Amazon had paid in taxes over the prior decade. (Mackenzie Scott would soon thereafter upstage her former husband by giving away more than $14 billion of her fortune in a series of donations that shook the NGO world. "MacKenzie Scott's Money Bombs Are Single Handedly Reshaping America," declared Bloomberg.)[37] But welcome as the funding may be for the nonprofits that receive some of the largesse, giant philanthropic grants from a tiny number of wealthy benefactors amount to a concentration of political influence that looks very much like oligarchy. As Carl Rhodes, the author of *Woke Capitalism*, has argued, this ruling-class advocacy "is not just about maintaining legitimacy, preventing revolt and forestalling regulation; it is about the direct takeover of democracy, both ideologically and practically."[38]

Nowhere is the desire for that takeover more visible than in corporate America's ongoing courtship of both major political parties. Though big business has traditionally enjoyed its coziest relationship with the Republican Party, plenty of investors and executives have recently shown themselves perfectly willing to anger or alienate GOP culture warriors by professing support for causes like abortion or LGBTQ rights, ostensibly because they also have plenty of friends and sympathizers in the Democratic Party. For instance, in 2022, the investment firm

BlackRock—which has come under fire from Republicans for its public positions on climate change, among other issues—doled out nearly $650,000 in campaign contributions to both Republicans *and* Democrats.[39] One of their top recipients was Democratic senator Chuck Schumer, who praised the company and sang the gospel of market fundamentalism the following year when Republican legislators introduced a bill designed to prohibit pension fund managers from using ESG criteria when deciding where to invest money. "Investing in a free-market economy involves choice," Schumer wrote in the *Wall Street Journal*. "The present rule gives investment managers an option. The Republican rule, on the other hand, ties investors' hands."[40] Even as 70 percent of Democratic voters in a 2021 survey agreed that neoliberalism had failed Americans, stakeholder capitalism was alluring enough for one of the most powerful Democrats in the nation to advocate once again for unshackling the market.[41]

The Trouble with Equity

For progressives, the crescendo of corporate interest in social justice, particularly during 2020's racial reckoning, has amounted only to a cynical co-optation of radical grassroots movements. "Rather than redistribution, redress, or reparations," one *Nation* contributor wrote of the corporate response to the reckoning, "corporate America and the political elite alike embraced the language of identity to assure those making radical demands in the streets that political change might just come one chief diversity officer at a time."[42]

It's true, on one hand, that business leaders have been far more amenable to measures like diversifying corporate boards and instituting companywide antibias trainings than they have been to some of the more confrontational slogans that arose from the protests—the call to abolish the police, for example. But on the other, 2020's reckoning also revealed that line between "corporate" antiracism and "radical" antiracism is often very fuzzy indeed. There have, for instance, been a number of steadfast calls for reparations from the business sector that don't look terribly different from what activists themselves have demanded. In 2020, Robert Johnson, the billionaire founder of BET, called for the federal government to pay $14 trillion in reparations to black Americans—the same figure included in several congressional reparations bills, including one introduced by progressive Cori Bush in 2023.[43] The CEO of the private equity firm Vista Equity, which is valued at $96 billion, likewise said in an interview that he believed corporations with historical ties to the slave trade also had an obligation to pay reparations.[44]

In 2022, major corporations also joined forces with progressive activists to throw their weight behind preserving affirmative action in higher education, which was eventually overturned by the conservative-majority Supreme Court. Prior to the ruling, nearly eighty blue chip firms—including Mastercard, JetBlue, Ikea, and Silicon Valley giants Google, Meta, and Apple—had filed a brief with the court expressing their enthusiastic support for Harvard's right to consider applicants' racial identities in its admissions process. Elite universities like Harvard were vital talent pipelines to elite corporations, the companies noted, and therefore had to be racially diverse in order for the leading firms to cultivate their own diverse workforces. ("Racial and ethnic diversity enhance business performance," the brief further argued.)[45] It was a stance that drew praise from a variety of racial justice groups, including the Legal Defense Fund—a civil rights organization founded in 1940 by Thurgood Marshall—which declared in a public statement that it was "proud to stand" with the corporate signatories of the brief.[46]

These instances of ideological alignment between activists and wealthy corporations aren't only coincidences. Even more insidious than the possibility of corporate America defanging radical antiracism is the fact that the contemporary ruling class is completely at ease with a vision of justice that overlaps with one held by progressives. Today that vision is most commonly called racial equity. And while for corporate America racial equity generally means diversifying their C-suites or subsidizing black entrepreneurship whereas for grassroots organizations racial equity is more likely to mean ending the disproportionate incarceration and police killings of black people, the two find common ground in an outsized focus on racial disparities.

For proponents of racial equity, the underrepresentation of black (and brown) people at the top of society (say, the Forbes billionaires list) and overrepresentation at the bottom (among the incarcerated or those living in poverty) is a sign of the enduring power of racism in the US. That's the argument advanced by Ibram X. Kendi, the country's foremost writer and speaker on antiracism. In his bestselling book *How to Be an*

Antiracist, which appears on countless reading lists and training guides, Kendi explains that racial equity exists "when two
or more racial groups are standing on a relatively equal footing" and offers the following example: In 2014, while only 41
percent of blacks and 45 percent of Latinos owned the homes
they lived in, 71 percent of white families owned theirs. "An
example of racial equity," Kendi writes, "would be if there
were relatively equitable percentages of all three racial groups
living in owner-occupied homes in the forties, seventies, or,
better, nineties."[47] A racially equitable society, in other words,
is simply one in which racial disparities have been eliminated.

Yet, as the professors Walter Benn Michaels and Adolph
Reed Jr. have argued, ensuring that equal percentages of every
racial group have identical access to society's resources (such
as, following Kendi's example, a private ownership-based
housing market) has nothing to do with changing an economy
that exploits the many for the enrichment of the few. A fixation on racial disparities as a sign of an abstract "systemic" or
"structural" racism furthermore obscures the very political
economy that generates society's grotesque inequalities in
the first place. "Every time racial disparity is invoked as the
lens through which to see American inequality," Reed and
Michaels write, "the overwhelming role played by the increased
inequality in the American class system is made invisible."[48]
What underpins the call for racial equity is the presumption
that America's current lopsided distribution of wealth and
resources would be justified so long as these disparities were
eliminated—that is, it would be acceptable if the top 1 percent
of the population held 90 percent of the nation's wealth just

so long as that 1 percent were (following the demographic makeup of the US population) 13 percent black, 18 percent Hispanic, and so on.

And the business sector has wholeheartedly celebrated the idea of racial equity because this project of eliminating racial disparities from American life ultimately doesn't much affect either their political dominance or their profit margins. Just ask the Wall Street founders of the financial services company Percapita, who consulted books like *How to Be An Antiracist* when brainstorming a business model that might help ameliorate long-standing racial disparities in finance and banking while also making them some money.[49] The firm landed on the goal of financial inclusion, or providing financial services to black and Latino people who, as the company noted, were disproportionately underserved. ("What could we build that would be just and equitable? How could we create a sustainable engine of change to remove the barriers so many face in achieving financial stability?" asks the group's official website.)[50] Likewise, just a few short years after the racial reckoning, a Bloomberg report found that corporate America had fulfilled its commitment to antiracism in at least one respect: Of the 300,000 workers that companies in the S&P 100 had hired between 2020 and 2021, 94 percent had been people of color.[51] And while most of these hires had been in lower-level positions, the proportion of non-white employees had increased significantly at higher ranking professional and managerial roles too. "Even at the executive level, more than half the added jobs went to workers of color," Bloomberg noted.

Because racial equity is a framework that demands only

that no particular racial group is *disproportionately* subject to hardship under the broader economic system, it's also one that political elites have eagerly brandished to avoid confronting the scarcity created by capitalism and instead advocating only for rearranging that scarcity. In 2020, the concept of racial equity was swiftly taken up by legislators and funders hoping to coax new life into neoliberal policy aims, who were, in fact, so partial to the notion that they insisted on swapping it for the idea of *equality*. On the campaign trail, Kamala Harris released a short animated video stressing the importance of equity over equality in policymaking.[52] "There's a big difference between equality and equity," she said in the video. "Equality suggests, 'Oh, everyone should get the same amount.' The problem with that [is] not everyone's starting out from the same place." *Equity*, she went on to explain, was a way of apportioning assistance based on need. This distinction also found a home among liberal nonprofit circles; as one California-based foundation insisted, equity "recognizes that due to racial or social status some communities need more help than others to achieve the same outcomes."[53]

But despite advocates' claims that the concept of equity addresses and corrects historical injustices that a traditional notion of equality somehow overlooks, a second look at this supposedly new framework suggests that we already have a perfectly good policy term for the process of determining who deserves assistance and who doesn't. That term is means-testing, and the practice also happens to be the preferred model of administering social welfare under neoliberalism.

Means-testing entails limiting benefits to a targeted group, traditionally those below a certain income cutoff, and its champions—like those of equity—have claimed that the practice ensures fairness. (In 2016, for instance, Hillary Clinton dismissed Bernie Sanders's call for tuition-free public college with the quip, "I am not in favor of making college free for Donald Trump's kids.")[54] But this conception of fairness tends to undermine the very programs means-testing is theoretically meant to enhance. For one thing, because means-tested programs must constantly monitor recipients' eligibility, they reliably generate byzantine and expensive bureaucracies that limit participation even among those who qualify. Legislators who want to shave down the social safety net often make administrative hurdles onerous by design; after all, the more red tape there is choking a program, the more people there are who are discouraged from using it. This also means that such programs are inefficient and politically unpopular: Those who qualify for means-tested benefits often aren't aware that they do or find themselves ill-equipped to slog through the necessary paperwork. And those who *don't* qualify for benefits but believe they're footing the bill with their taxes can come to harbor resentment for such programs.

In this context, it's easy to understand why so many elites today have warmed to the concept of equity: It's a convenient euphemism for the continuation of neoliberal economics with a progressive twist. (Old-fashioned "equality," on the other hand, sounds rather like the kind of universalism that legislators on both sides of the aisle have worked to sweep off the table for decades.) Racial equity is a perfectly acceptable model of redistribution for our contemporary ruling class because it treats things like decent jobs, education, and health care as limited resources that only need to be divided up proportionally by race, not as public goods to be expanded and improved for all.

The language of equity makes it that much easier to cloak this revamped means-testing in moral righteousness, but at a moment when working-class Americans, regardless of race, face a declining standard of living, it's a zero-sum approach that amounts only to slicing up a shrinking pie in a slightly different way. As historian Touré Reed has argued, while anti-discrimination policies still serve as a much-needed bulwark against racism in the labor market, they can only truly improve life for the majority of black Americans within a type of economy that has been nonexistent for at least a generation. "If the US economy were still characterized today by an expanding middle class, anti-discrimination measures alone might be a reasonable fix," Reed has said. "The problem is that the game has changed."[55]

The game was changed most notably by the onset of deindustrialization and the subsequent evaporation of high-wage blue-collar jobs beginning in the middle of the twentieth century. By the 1960s, the civil rights leader Bayard Rustin had predicted that shifts underway in the economy—namely, the rise of automation and the erosion of manual labor occupations—would render civil rights legislation toothless in the long run if left unaddressed. "We are in the midst of a technological revolution which is altering the fundamental structure of the labor force, destroying unskilled and semi-skilled jobs—jobs in which Negroes are disproportionately concentrated," Rustin wrote in 1964.[56] Without a significant overhaul of the structure of labor in the US and a raft of public programs to guarantee full employment, housing, and education, he argued, the civil rights movement itself would soon run up against its limits.

His warning was prescient. As Judith Stein would show in her sweeping account *Running Steel, Running America,* the collapse of domestic manufacturing over the latter half of the twentieth century would, in effect, undercut the measures against employment discrimination established under Title VII of the Civil Rights Act of 1964. Though Title VII legally prohibited employers from engaging in racial discrimination and thereby helped increase the *percentage* of blacks working within certain occupations, the simultaneous disappearance of jobs in steel and adjacent industries over the next several decades meant that, in many cases, the total *number* of black workers in those fields would decline dramatically. Between 1974 and 1988, for instance, representation of black workers in the electrical trades increased from around 5 percent to a little over 8 percent. But, Stein noted, "it would be difficult to call this progress, because the number of black electricians declined from 718 to 431."[57]

Today the family-sustaining blue-collar manufacturing jobs that helped forge a black middle class during the civil rights era are long gone, replaced by an expansive low-wage service sector and fewer and fewer avenues to long-term economic security for most working people. And while racism and discrimination still shamefully circumscribe the lives of many, the unrelenting downward pressure on the vast majority of Americans of all races suggests that measures intended to ensure that certain racial groups aren't disproportionately subject to precarity—as opposed to measures seeking to eliminate, or at least ameliorate, that precarity—will continually struggle to win popular support.

To put it another way, calls for racial equity in the current economic pressure cooker—whether from corporations or activist organizations—have amounted to little more than calls to diversify the shrinking ranks of those lucky enough to escape downward mobility. And this project is one that's completely compatible with the interests of business elites, neoliberal politicians, and wealthy philanthropists. If the protests of 2020 had ignited a wide-scale cultural reckoning over race that captured the nation, the seamless incorporation of that reckoning into the economic order also suggested there was nothing about it that the ruling class found objectionable in the least.

2

HOW ANTIRACISM BECAME A GIFT TO BOSSES

The sprawling, unregulated industry that exists to monitor and manage the racial biases of American workers is now worth somewhere between 3 and 8 billion dollars, which is, for comparison, at least ten times the budget of the National Labor Relations Board, the federal agency that oversees and enforces labor laws for every workplace in the country.[1] Today this vast wing of human resources management is typically called diversity, equity, and inclusion, or DEI, but it's a testament to its infinite adaptability (and lack of any official industry standards or oversight) that permutations abound, including D&I (diversity and inclusion), DEIB (diversity, equity, inclusion, and belonging), and even JEDI (justice, equity, diversity, and inclusion). One marketing firm has projected that global spending on these services could reach $15.4 billion by 2026.[2]

The contemporary DEI complex comprises a dizzying array of personnel and products. C-suite DEI officers and university DEI administrators collect six-figure salaries to manage in-house diversity initiatives and keep their employers in compliance with antidiscrimination law; third-party consultants lead company-wide antiracism trainings and coach CEOs on recovering from race-related public relations gaffes. The most prestigious DEI practitioners include former ACLU director Laura Murphy, who conducted a two-year-long civil rights audit for Facebook; on the crunchier end are groups like Aorta, a worker-owned "anti-oppression resource and training alliance" that offers guided workshops like "Uprooting White Supremacy" for businesses and NGOs alike. In the digital era, companies like Syndio—which counts General Mills, Nordstrom, and Volvo among its clients—now offer platforms that track the demographic data of employees in order to monitor whether companies' HR practices are sufficiently "equitable."

During 2020's racial reckoning, demand for DEI exploded. That year alone, according to Bloomberg, the number of managerial-level DEI positions in the US tripled.[3] Consultants whose businesses had been struggling at the start of the pandemic suddenly found themselves fielding dozens, even hundreds, of requests for training. Crossroads, a Chicago-based group that has conducted antiracism trainings since 2000, said it had received 275 inquiries in June of 2020, around ten times its typical monthly average of twenty-five to thirty inquiries.[4] "Right now company leadership is realizing that dismantling racism is a good investment in our future," a spokesperson said of the spike in demand. Even the federal government under the newly elected Joe Biden rushed to roll out new DEI measures: In the spring of 2021, the State Department appointed its first-ever chief diversity and inclusion officer; shortly after that, the Defense Department named a deputy inspector general for diversity and inclusion.[5] (In the UK, following a scandalous Oprah interview in which Meghan Markle tearfully discussed the racism she had experienced at Buckingham Palace, the British monarchy also dutifully announced it was considering the hire of a diversity chief.)[6]

Lost in the crescendo of DEI pledges was the fact that several of the most popular and widely used DEI initiatives simply don't work, at least not in the way they're advertised. Mandatory workplace antiracism trainings, for instance, surged in popularity in tandem with the protests. But even though they're now used by major companies including Target, the *New York Times,* Sephora, and Penguin Random House (which assigned one of its own books, *How to Be an Antiracist,* to all employees in its "first-ever true company-wide read" in 2020), the most rigorous studies to date have shown that these types of compulsory trainings don't do much to change people's biases and, in some cases, even engrain them more deeply. According to the available evidence, they also largely fail to increase workplace diversity or improve employee morale. As sociologists Frank Dobbin and Alexandra Kalev have concluded, "Diversity training is likely the most expensive, and least effective, diversity program around."[7]

Title VII and the Birth of DEI

When it comes to the promise of stamping out racial bias among employees, the multibillion-dollar DEI apparatus rests on a shaky foundation. Research dating back to the 1930s has indicated that perennially popular initiatives like mandatory sensitivity or antiracism trainings usually don't alter people's prejudices. In what's likely the most comprehensive investigation of such trainings to date, Dobbin and Kalev surveyed more than three decades of data on DEI programs collected from over 800 firms and found that they not only failed to reduce workers' prejudices, but even *exacerbated* biases and left participants hostile. "Trainers tell us that people often respond to compulsory courses with anger and resistance—and many participants actually report more animosity toward other groups afterward," they wrote.[8]

Other studies on such trainings have found that even in the rare cases where these sessions do manage to lower participants' biases, the effects are fleeting and don't alter people's attitudes over the long term. The more quixotic interventions that have shown promise—such as one 2012 experiment that successfully lowered participants' biases through a twelve-week-long college-level course on racism and discrimination—aren't appropriate or feasible for most workplaces.[9] Nor do they necessarily convert those who aren't already predisposed to ridding themselves of prejudice: As the authors of the 2012 study noted, the experiment was most effective on the participants who were concerned about discrimination even prior to the course and diligently completed all the exercises assigned to them.

If commonplace DEI trainings don't work as they're advertised, why exactly have companies continued to pour billions of dollars into the industry that peddles them? One reason, of course, is that flashily spending money on DEI initiatives helps generate positive press for corporations, particularly those whose reputations have been marred by past discrimination scandals or lawsuits. Ramping up DEI also affords businesses some additional legal protection against potential future discrimination lawsuits, since courts have generally considered the presence of DEI programs sufficient evidence that a company has taken active steps to prevent or address discrimination or workplace harassment. And as Ivy League universities and other elite educational institutions increasingly prioritize racial justice themselves, DEI programs can help attract highly credentialed job candidates hoping to work for firms that share their values.

Corporate America's interest in DEI, though, isn't limited to window-dressing or rote legal compliance. What DEI initiatives offer employers is not only the immediate boost of flattering press and protection from liability but, perhaps more crucially, an increasingly useful way to deepen managerial control and flex soft power over employees. DEI, as a cornerstone of contemporary stakeholder capitalism, increases employer and private sector discretion and, in its most uncompromising forms, preempts labor unrest by fracturing workforces behind a PR-friendly veil.

One important (if largely unspoken) way in which DEI serves the interests of business is that unlike labor laws or workplace safety regulations, it isn't subject to any kind of meaningful government oversight. Employers that expose their workers to dangerous working conditions can face fines and other penalties from the Occupational Health and Safety Administration; likewise, companies that have illegally interfered with workers' attempts to unionize or have wrongfully terminated employees can be ordered by the National Labor Relations Board to reinstate fired personnel and pay back wages. DEI, on the other hand, is entirely controlled and administered by employers themselves, which means that (among other advantages) there aren't any real consequences for companies that set DEI benchmarks like hiring targets or pay equity but then fail to meet them.

This high degree of employer autonomy has, in fact, been the bedrock of private-sector antidiscrimination efforts since the 1960s. Title VII of the 1964 Civil Rights Act prohibited discrimination by "race, color, religion, sex, or national origin" in the private sector and called on employers to establish "equal employment opportunities" for all workers. Yet, as Frank Dobbin explains in his book *Inventing Equal Opportunity*, while Title VII made discrimination illegal and urged employers to take "affirmative action" to combat it, it simultaneously failed either to define discrimination explicitly or provide meaningful guidance as to what affirmatively eliminating that discrimination should look like. The government, in Dobbin's words, had "outlawed discrimination without saying what it was."[10]

Title VII had additionally taken shape as an alternative to the so-called Humphrey Bill, a competing piece of legislation that sought to ameliorate discrimination against black workers within a broader employment program that not only empowered the Labor Department to adjudicate discrimination complaints but also established new public sector jobs and training programs for workers. As historian Judith Stein noted, this bill was championed by a number of labor and civil rights leaders, including A. Philip Randolph, who believed that the disproportionate unemployment of black workers was a consequence of the ongoing disappearance of industrial jobs, not simply the result of racial discrimination. The jobs-focused Humphrey Bill, Stein wrote, "sent an intellectual message that black unemployment was not simply a problem of human relations, where morality and democracy demanded the abolition of actions based upon prejudice, but was a function of the changing labor market."[11]

That more comprehensive proposal, however, faced a steep uphill political battle and was ultimately set aside by policymakers and advocates in the ensuing political fracas over civil rights legislation. Title VII—the antidiscrimination statute that would pass in lieu of the Humphrey Bill—was not only narrower in scope, but also drastically curtailed the federal government's ability to fight private sector discrimination. While Title VII had established a federal Equal Employment Opportunity Commission to oversee workplace equal opportunity compliance, congressional Republicans and southern Democrats had fiercely resisted granting the EEOC the authority or reach of an agency like the National Labor Relations Board. The final version of the Civil Rights Act gave the EEOC the power to investigate discrimination complaints and help mediate disputes but no real means to enforce Title VII or punish violations. Combined with the vagueness of the antidiscrimination mandate, the lack of meaningful federal mechanisms to enforce equal opportunity hiring in the private sector meant that businesses—and specifically, their human resources departments—were left to devise their own policies and practices around preventing workplace discrimination and ensuring equal opportunity compliance. And absent a muscular government agency to enforce the law, workers were left to sort out any racial discrimination they encountered by suing offending employers in civil court.

As Dobbin argues, in this typically American brew of political hostility to federal regulations and a self-sabotaging state, the private sector was, in essence, positioned to create the very antidiscrimination standards that it was expected to comply with, and as a result, the policies developed by the leading firms in the US over the next decades would come to shape government standards, rather than the other way around. If the Civil Rights Act had enshrined an obligation for employers to combat discrimination, the *practice* of equal employment opportunity—or what would come to be known as diversity management and then DEI—has been less a triumph of government policy than a byproduct of capitalist enterprise. Over the next several decades, human resources professionals and management publications would together fill the vacuum generated by the ambiguities of Title VII by developing the antidiscrimination and diversity programs we know today. The most notable of these practices included establishing entire affirmative action or equal opportunity offices in workplaces—the direct precursors to today's DEI departments. "It was politicians who outlawed discrimination in private employment," Dobbin writes. "But it was personnel managers who defined what job discrimination was and was not."[12]

In the 1980s, the Reagan administration would further entrench the private sector's jurisdiction over antidiscrimination by spurning the concept of affirmative action and cutting funding to an already feeble Equal Employment Opportunity Commission. Human resources personnel, who subsequently found themselves under pressure to justify their jobs under the conservative regime, swiftly rebranded workplace equal opportunity programs as "diversity management" and began touting diversity as a free market value that would enhance businesses performance and drive up worker productivity. And though progressives today might assume that corporations at the time were delighted to abandon equal opportunity measures with Reagan's blessing, business leaders in fact openly contested Reagan's attack on workplace affirmative action. Nearly half a century before leading corporations would oppose the overturning of affirmative action in higher education, America's top executives doubled down on their efforts to preserve antidiscrimination initiatives in the private sector. Despite Reagan's cuts to the EEOC, Dobbin notes, a 1986 survey of Fortune 500 companies found that "nine out of 10 planned no changes to affirmative action programs and the tenth planned to expand them."[13]

Why Bosses Love DEI

The business case for diversity began with Gary Becker, a University of Chicago economist and Milton Friedman protege who argued in the 1950s that discrimination was bad for business.[14] Refusing to hire someone based on their race, gender, or anything other than their aptitude for the job, Becker said, would inevitably hurt companies financially over the long run by pushing up the cost of labor. In Becker's view, a market left to regulate itself would eventually eliminate discrimination simply by making bigotry unprofitable.

Today, in the spirit of Becker, the most powerful capitalist lobbies and organizations agree on antidiscrimination as a good business practice and extoll the importance of DEI measures in the workplace. In recent years, the Chamber of Commerce, the Business Roundtable, and the World Economic Forum have all assembled reports and coalitions dedicated to achieving racial equity in the workplace.[15] The influential McKinsey firm likewise provides extensive coaching and resources for major corporations looking to build up their DEI programs. "The business case for diversity is robust, and the relationship between diversity on executive teams and the likelihood of financial outperformance has gotten stronger over time," reads an official McKinsey guide on DEI.[16]

This vision of antidiscrimination as an accelerant for profit has in turn fertilized a diversity management cottage industry that has only grown larger every year since Reagan's attack on affirmative action the '80s. (McKinsey estimates that the number of DEI positions in the US grew fourfold just between 2017 and 2022.)[17] Over the years professionals have traded the Civil Rights–era label of equal opportunity for diversity and, more recently, for DEI, but the biggest companies have held surprisingly steadfast in their commitment to such initiatives. Today every Fortune 500 employer in the US has antidiscrimination policies in place, initiatives that range from diversity hiring targets to required antiracism training for employees to codified discrimination grievance procedures.[18] Nearly every company in the S&P 100 employs a chief DEI officer; 75 percent have recruitment programs with HBCUs.[19] The contemporary zeal for DEI is so widespread that, even despite its lackluster track record, some elite workforces have demanded more of it from their employers. Staffers at the *New York Times*, for example, released a public memo in 2020 that called for the creation of a "C-level diversity position" and "mandatory and regular" antiracism trainings for all of the paper's employees.[20]

According to its advocates, DEI not only makes companies more profitable but also fosters friendlier, more collegial workplaces for people of color, women, and others who may face discrimination or prejudice, which in turn boosts worker morale and retention. "If we don't have employees that understand people of different cultures, different backgrounds—companies are going to find themselves losing good employees to discriminatory practices," one DEI professional told ABC News.[21] Public opinion polling has confirmed that most American workers also like the idea of workplace policies to combat discrimination and ensure fairness in hiring, pay, and promotions.[22]

But to what extent has the DEI industry actually helped to engender the kind of congenial workplace relations that Americans want? While many DEI professionals may genuinely want to help underrepresented workers, these good intentions tend to run up against the fact that it's more often than not employers—rather than their employees—who reap the greatest rewards of DEI. For one thing, DEI initiatives rely on the existing workplace hierarchy to function and, in many cases, even more deeply entrench that pecking order. Mandatory antiracism trainings—even when they come about as the result of an earnest desire to reduce racial prejudice—expand employers' capacity to surveil and discipline employees by demanding access to their thoughts and feelings on highly charged topics and then evaluating those employees' responses, often with the explicit goal of generating unease and prompting deference. ("Embracing discomfort and humility along the way will enable your growth as an ally," reads one DEI training guide used by Disney.)[23] Some DEI consultants—most notably *White Fragility* author Robin DiAngelo—have pointed to the discord these trainings can generate as just more proof of how badly workers need reeducation. But as Dobbin and Kalev have noted, people tend to dislike others' attempts to change their thoughts or infringe on their behavior: "Try to coerce me to do X, Y, or Z, and I'll do the opposite just to prove that I'm my own person," they've explained.[24] When the same manager who dispenses your paycheck and decides whether to promote you or fire you is also monitoring you for signs of latent prejudice, it's little wonder that people feel some defensiveness, if not outright hostility.

Corporations whose ruthless business practices have exacerbated the very society-wide racial inequalities they vehemently condemned in 2020 have also used DEI trainings to offload some of the embarrassment associated with racism—and the responsibility for ameliorating it—onto their employees. Bank of America, for instance, spent the years leading up to the Great Recession trading securities backed by risky mortgages and engaging in predatory lending, particularly to black and Hispanic home buyers.[25] According to the think tank People's Policy Project, the housing crash that resulted from their and other financial institutions playing fast and loose with subprime mortgages led to a twenty-fold increase in the percentage of black homeowners with underwater mortgages.[26]

Though it was, of course, Bank of America's top brass—not its bank tellers, customer service reps, or other rank-and-file employees—that helped engineer the housing bubble that led to the 2008 foreclosure crisis, when it came time to demonstrate its commitment to antiracism, those same executives had little to say about their own culpability. Instead, bank leaders enrolled the company in a training series called the Racial Equity 21-Day Challenge, a three-week DEI education course on systemic racism, intersectionality, and white privilege, among other topics.[27] Bank of America employees across the nation were urged to participate. "Individually and collectively, we must continue to confront our country's history and relationship to identity," the training module instructed participants.[28] That appeal to collectivity was an opportune sleight of hand that allowed Bank of America's leadership to volunteer their underlings to perform antiracist penance on behalf of the whole company.

Even workers who support efforts to battle discrimination or increase workplace diversity can find themselves baffled by these aggressive pushes from the C-suite for antiracism education when rank-and-file employees are, after all, largely not the people responsible for the direction of the company. Ted, a software engineer who works at a tech company based on the East Coast, said he'd always been concerned about the lack of diversity at his office and welcomed a reassessment of the company's hiring policies. But at the height of 2020's protests, his employer—like others eager to institute new, aggressive-sounding DEI measures—started pressing employees to attend a series of company-sponsored antiracism workshops. At the encouragement of his supervisor, Ted sat in on a seminar where a consultant explained that microaggressions—indirect or subtle slights against racial minorities—reproduced "past historic injustices" such as the "enslavement of Africans, the Holocaust, and the taking away of land from Indigenous peoples." In the workplace, the speaker said, the dissemination of these miniature traces of genocide and slavery were "*constant* and *continual* without an end date."

Well-intentioned as the session may have been, its focus on employees' individual and possibly unconscious actions seemed to Ted like a convenient way for the company to shift the responsibility for the problem of a lack of racial diversity at the company away from those in charge of hiring and onto regular employees. "Since the seminar, I've talked to hiring managers several times about increasing the number of women and people of color on staff," he said. "And nothing ever really seems to happen." A few months after the training, he submitted a question to management asking whether the seminars had increased diversity or otherwise improved the percentage of underrepresented groups in the engineering department. There was no answer.

For employers, in other words, part of the appeal of contemporary DEI education programs rife with activist vocabulary is that a little jargon and conceptual fuzziness easily become progressive smokescreens for those who want to avoid committing company leadership to anything concrete. In fact, the more arcane or activist-inflected the DEI rhetoric is, the more certain executives have gravitated to it: "You can make a lot of money in diversity being abstract," one longtime DEI consultant told the outlet the Cut in 2021.[29] "I'll say, 'You really need to look at your insurance policies and how you're giving out rates.' Clients will say, 'I ain't going to mess with that. Let's talk about allyship. Let's talk about white fragility—that'd be a great topic.'"

At their worst, these types of trainings aren't just ineffective or diversionary: They also have the potential to turn explicitly punitive. In 2018, the private liberal arts school Smith College used DEI trainings to crack down on support staff in response to a public scandal in which a black student accused a janitor of calling campus security on her while she'd been eating lunch.[30] Though the recorded encounter between the student and the campus security had been civil—and a subsequent third-party investigation concluded that no discrimination had taken place—the incident, which initially looked like an instance of racial profiling, swiftly attracted the attention of the national media. In an attempt to defray the mounting controversy, administrators put the accused janitor on leave and rushed out a raft of new DEI measures, including installing a Vice President of Equity and Inclusion and mandating antiracism training.

That training, however, was required only of staffers—hourly employees largely drawn from the working-class neighborhoods around Smith—and not of the school's professors. According to several of the college's employees who spoke to the *New York Times* in 2021, the trainings were uncomfortable, psychologically invasive affairs that "left workers cynical."[31] Jodi Shaw, a Smith alumna who worked for the school, quit her job after a mandatory three-day "professional development retreat," which included a session dedicated to exploring employees' racial identities. "I was troubled by the thought of having to discuss my identity because I don't really come to work to engage in therapy or comb through past traumas or talk about religion or politics or anything," Shaw said in a video she posted online after the training.[32] "I really just come to work to do my job." But when she voiced this discomfort during the training, she said, the consultants running the training pointedly told the group, "When a white person says they're uncomfortable talking about race, you should know that what they're expressing is not actually discomfort—it's called white fragility, and it's a power play." Shaw said that she considered this upbraiding a "public, intentional humiliation."

Right-wing media outlets soon picked up the story and Shaw attracted controversy after appearing on then Fox anchor Tucker Carlson's show to discuss the incident.[33] But while Carlson and other conservatives seized upon her account as proof that universities were running Marxist indoctrination sessions, the Smith incident was, in most ways, the exact opposite of "Workers of the world unite." What the fiasco revealed most vividly was rather the sweeping power that employers hold over their employees and the new avenues by which they're leveraging and consolidating that power.

In the typical American workplace, even theoretically progressive antiracism trainings that are administered from the top down and used to evaluate employees will almost always put workers of all races at a disadvantage. Aside from providing just one more opportunity for bosses to scrutinize employees for signs of insubordination or "attitude" problems, the pop-psychology-based concepts that frequently turn up in these trainings—implicit bias, microaggressions, white fragility—are slippery enough to serve as non-falsifiable pretexts for disciplining employees. At Smith, even after the employees accused of racial profiling were cleared of wrongdoing by a third party, president Kathleen McCartney justified her suspension of the janitor involved and her continuation of mandatory training by stating, "It is impossible to rule out the potential role of implicit racial bias."[34] From a managerial perspective, it's infinitely useful if "implicit racial bias" is grounds for discipline and a worker (even one exonerated by an independent investigation) can't ever quite prove they don't have it.

Deploying such vaporous concepts in the workplace furthermore helps obscure the reality of employment in the US, in which the most immediate and egregious inequality is the one between employer and employee. While it's illegal to abuse an employee on the basis of their race, gender, or sexuality, it's mostly legal to treat a worker terribly because they're a worker. The political philosopher Elizabeth Anderson has argued that this is the inevitable consequence of the at-will employment contract, which governs the vast majority of workplaces in the US and ensures that employers can fire employees for any reason (or no reason whatsoever), barring only a small handful of exceptions.[35] What this exhaustive discretion amounts to, Anderson argues, is that, in practice, private employers wield more power over their employees than the US government does over its citizens. Employers can (and do) dictate how workers dress, what they're allowed to say on social media, even what they do with their free time. It's perfectly legal and commonplace, she notes, for employers to surveil workers' communications, order them to undergo medical testing, or punish them for their political preferences. At-will law allows Tyson Foods to refuse its poultry-plant workers bathroom breaks and Apple to search the personal belongings of its retail staff daily. "If the U.S. government imposed such regulations on us," Anderson points out, "we would rightly protest that our constitutional rights were being violated."[36]

In this context, mandatory antiracism trainings become another way for employers to monitor—if not outright intimidate—workers, all while appearing tough on racism in the public eye. Managers have openly admitted as much: In the *Harvard Business Review*, which has influenced the trajectory of DEI best practices since the '60s, one executive advised not only requiring all employees to attend antiracism training but also making their job security at least partially contingent on the results of that antiracist education.[37] "Our annual staff performance reviews hold every staff member accountable for achievement against a personal racial equity and inclusion objective at the beginning of the year," he wrote. Another contributor to the publication similarly recommended that companies "adopt a no-tolerance-for-racism policy like Franklin Templeton's, which led to its swift termination of Amy Cooper," the white woman who notoriously called the police on a black birdwatcher in Central Park in 2020.[38]

Difficult as it may be to summon much sympathy for Cooper herself, it's also clear that employers' ability to fire people for their conduct outside of work has already taken a serious toll on American workers' rights. The sociologist Arne Kalleberg, who studies precarious work in an international context, has suggested that one reason the official rates of temp work are lower in the United States than they are in Europe is that the pervasive nature of at-will employment in the US essentially renders even "permanent" workers temporary in practice since they can be fired at any moment and without any specific cause.[39] The last thing the corrosive at-will arrangement needs at this moment (or any other) is a new progressive gloss. Or to put it another way, making it easier or more widely acceptable for bosses to oust or discipline racists isn't much of a win for workers when the boss remains the ultimate arbiter of who exactly counts as racist.

That particular discretionary power briefly became national policy in July of 2020, when the Trump-appointed National Labor Relations Board (NLRB) ruled in favor of allowing employers to fire workers trying to unionize if those workers were deemed to have used "racist" or "profane" speech in their union-related activity, ending nearly seventy years of precedent protecting union representatives' right to use heated language during grievance procedures or other confrontations with management.[40] In a statement on the ruling, NLRB chairman John Ring claimed that the decision had been rendered in service of antidiscrimination. "For too long, the Board has protected employees who engage in obscene, racist, and sexually harassing speech not tolerated in almost any workplace today," he said.[41] "Our decision . . . ends this unwarranted protection, eliminates the conflict between the NLRA [National Labor Relations Act] and antidiscrimination laws, and acknowledges that the expectations for employee conduct in the workplace have changed."

In fact, in the case that had prompted the ruling, nothing that a reasonable person would have recognized as racist speech had occurred; rather, a black General Motors employee had "mockingly acted a caricature of a slave" to challenge a manager's demand for subservience. Fighting racism was simply the thin pretext for a pro-employer NLRB to grease the wheels for bosses trying to sack union troublemakers. But the decision had come down in the thick of 2020's reckoning, and the same liberal media outlets and progressive advocacy groups that had painstakingly scrutinized and inveighed against every policy decision of the Trump administration were uniformly silent on the matter.

The Chamber of Commerce and employer-side labor lawyers, on the other hand, were delighted.[42] The law firm Ballard Spahr—whose services include "union avoidance training" and has counted among its clients several large universities fighting staff unionization efforts—wrote in an approving dispatch after the ruling, "Employers should welcome this change by the NLRB as it provides some clarity for employers seeking to discipline employees who engage in abusive or harassing conduct in the context of protected, concerted activity."[43]

The New Union Busting

For all the time and money spent on dubious DEI schemes, there already exists an incredibly reliable and effective mechanism for combating workplace discrimination, lowering racial prejudice among whites, and narrowing pay gaps between workers of different races or genders. Employers, however, have not only studiously avoided this time-tested fix but also spend millions each year to suppress it. That's because the fix is a union contract, or the very same mechanism that, by definition, curtails employers' power.

When it comes to workplace inequalities, unions have been one of the most consistent and successful means of shrinking pay disparities between men and women and between workers of different races. Study after study has confirmed not only that women and black workers in unions earn more on average than those who aren't unionized but that pay gaps by gender or race shrink significantly—and even outright disappear—within unionized workplaces, thanks to wage floors set by collective bargaining agreements.[44] In fact, unions have historically been so effective at guaranteeing a baseline of economic security for members that the relatively high rate of unionization among black workers in the postwar period helped create and sustain a black middle class. (The unfortunate corollary of this effect is that as union density has diminished over the past several decades, so have the fortunes of working-class households of all races.)

Unlike the mandatory antiracism trainings that have proliferated over the last several decades, unions even have an impressive record of reducing racial prejudice among workers.[45] One deceptively simple reason for this is that successful collective bargaining requires workers to bridge racial divides and other differences in order to win concessions from their employer, and working alongside fellow shop members in pursuit of these and other shared goals tends to generate mutual respect, if not genuine camaraderie. Dobbin's ongoing workplace research has also confirmed that having employees of different backgrounds work together toward a common goal appears to be a far more useful way of reducing bias in the workplace than subjecting them to tortuous trainings: "We know from a lot of social science research the way to get people to change their stereotypes about other groups is to have them work side by side with members of other groups as equals," he told Vox in 2018.[46]

But if unions consistently outperform the multibillion-dollar DEI industry on these and other so-called diversity measures, it's little surprise that companies prefer top-down DEI initiatives administered by HR departments to the idea of their employees engaging in collective bargaining. Unions, though far more effective at reducing racial and gender disparities and lowering individual prejudices in the workplace than DEI, also necessarily alter the balance of power between employer and employee, which is something that DEI departments, on the other hand, rely on and help entrench by design.

The current business enthusiasm for DEI is perhaps rivaled only by the business aversion to organized labor. Today the most powerful financial institutions in the US not only have DEI programs in place but have, between them, donated billions of dollars to racial justice causes. Yet, when the CEOs of the largest banks were asked at a 2021 Senate hearing whether they would remain neutral if their employees tried to unionize, not a single one said yes.[47] According to the Economic Policy Institute, American companies spend at least $400 million every year on union avoidance consulting, a figure that's staggering yet almost certainly an underestimate.[48] The watchdog groups that track union-busting expenditures rely on official documents that companies have filed with the Department of Labor, but thanks to lax enforcement of this reporting and the presence of numerous loopholes that allow union-avoidance consultants to avoid or delay filing, there exists a vast off-the-books world of union-busting activity that never makes it onto public record.

DEI itself, it turns out, may constitute yet another loophole through which companies can direct funds to union busters without drawing the scrutiny of the Department of Labor. The investigative reporter Lee Fang has shown that a growing number of employer-side attorneys and other union avoidance professionals have seamlessly moved into DEI management, often by combining the two into one expedient personnel package for employers.[49] "The reality is that many employers will be dealing with union organizing if they don't make a sincere effort to adhere to Diversity & Inclusion-related laws and principles," warns Projections Inc., a consulting firm that publishes a union avoidance resource unsubtly titled UnionProof.[50] "Frequent reminders that there is a no-tolerance policy for discriminatory behavior by any employee, including executives, is an excellent strategy for union avoidance as unions step up their unionization efforts through charges of workplace discrimination." Greer Consulting, a diversity management firm whose clients include Nike and Staples, promises that their services "can keep unionization at bay for years to come."[51] And plenty of in-house diversity officers now perform double duty as union busters: When the retailer REI learned of its workers' plans to form a union, its chief diversity officer issued a dispatch to employees explaining why a union wasn't the "right choice" for the company, prefaced appropriately with a land acknowledgement and a commitment to "racial equity." Diversity officers at Google and Dollar General, Fang notes, have likewise played key roles in suppressing budding organizing efforts by hiring and overseeing third-party union busters.

Employers, in other words, can quite comfortably leverage DEI as a business-friendly alternative to labor organizing. Take the common DEI practice of employee resource groups, or ERGs, which are meant to serve as support networks for underrepresented groups, usually racial or sexual minorities. Ninety percent of Fortune 500 companies today use ERGs; Google alone has more than sixteen designated groups for black employees, disabled employees, mixed-race employees, and transgender employees, among others. McKinsey advises companies to assemble thoughtful ERGs that can serve as vehicles for serious employee feedback on DEI issues: "Employees today are connecting their job to purpose like never before, and want to be part of the establishment and evolution of policies, practices, and procedures—especially when it comes to DEI," the firm noted in 2022.[52] "The opportunity for organizations is clear: to position their ERGs as sources of ideas and engines for change."

But the reason why ERGs are ideal "engines of change" for employers is that they don't threaten managerial power in any way and, at their most useful, even help stave off the threat of unionization. Union avoidance specialists have encouraged companies to adopt ERGs for this exact reason: "When employees believe they don't have a voice, they are going to turn to the union," warns Projections' UnionProof blog.[53] Among the firm's recommended tactics for adequately facilitating "employee voice" in order to preempt any rumblings of unionization? Open dialogue sessions between employees and executives, the creation of rigorous internal dispute resolution systems, and employee resource groups. Other corporate law firms have similarly advised employers to boost their DEI practices and corporate social responsibility programs to quell worker unrest. According to a lawyer at Vinson & Elkins—a firm Bloomberg Law once called a leader in DEI in the legal field—employers that welcomed employees' input on such matters were more "likely to decrease the likelihood of an organizing campaign, and probably be more profitable."[54]

By serving as manager-approved conduits—even pressure valves—for employee discontent, ERGs may be the closest thing we have today to so-called company unions, or workplace groups that theoretically operate for the benefit of workers but are organized and overseen by employers. In the early twentieth century, employers regularly established company unions to defang any budding labor militancy or calls to unionize among their workers. For example, when the black railroad car porters and maids employed by the famed Pullman Company attempted to organize for better working conditions in the 1920s, the firm formed a company union dubbed the Employee Representation Plan and (in a move that uncannily prefigured modern-day DEI practices) included black workers on the organization's board to demonstrate its forward-thinking on race relations. Despite this feint at sensitivity, however, the goal—and the ultimate effect—of the Pullman company union was to create divisions among the workers and thwart the formation of an actual union. This tactic remained effective until 1935, when the National Labor Relations Act outlawed company unions, finally allowing Pullman workers to defeat the company's vicious union busting and form the Brotherhood of Sleeping Car Porters, the first black labor union to receive official certification (and an eventual pipeline to the civil rights movement).

Modern-day ERGs function so similarly to this now-illegal practice that employer-side attorneys and human resources organizations have cautioned companies that without the appropriate guardrails in place, they could potentially run the risk of violating labor law. "ERG approval criteria and operating guidelines should expressly prohibit any ERG from 'negotiating' or addressing the 'terms and conditions' of employment," Jackson Lewis, a leading union avoidance law firm, has advised.[55] "ERGs are not unions and employers should have rules prohibiting ERGs from behaving like unions."

The public attention on racial justice in the summer of 2020 presented even more opportunities for business interests to seize upon hypothetically egalitarian rhetoric explicitly to undermine budding unionization efforts, particularly at workplaces known for attracting people inclined to progressive politics. In 2021, when staffers at the famously liberal broadcast channel MSNBC attempted to form a union, managers soberly informed staffers that union dues could hinder the company's efforts to diversify its staff. In a captive-audience meeting convened by management to dissuade workers from joining the union, one executive warned the assembled employees, "If our entry-level jobs come with . . . a requirement to write a check, pay a percentage of your salary—I'm desperately concerned that we might be turning away people who might be exactly the people that we want to be the next generation of MSNBC, NBC News employees."[56]

Of course, like any other style of union busting, the antiracist variant of labor suppression isn't always guaranteed to work. (Employees at MSNBC eventually voted to unionize in spite of their bosses' DEI-inflected attempts to prevent that very outcome.) But managers, in the end, only have to convince enough people of their noble intentions to tip the scales in a union election. The same year that MSNBC staffers won their union drive, warehouse workers at an Amazon plant in Bessemer, Alabama, lost theirs after a vicious and protracted union busting campaign in which Amazon's management (among other tactics) promised to redouble their efforts to address bias and discrimination on the job. One employee who ultimately voted down the union told the *New York Times* he "believed a commitment by management to improve the workplace over the next 100 days, a promise made during the company's campaign."[57] That employee, the paper noted, ultimately "joined other anti-union workers in pushing Amazon to better train employees and to educate managers on anti-bias techniques."

The DEI Ouroboros

The legitimacy (and longevity) of the DEI industry has rested on the assumption that making American workplaces hospitable to non-white workers, women, and other protected classes is an undertaking so complex that it requires the expertise of a coterie of professionals. But as Dobbin and Kalev's research suggests, the conditions that make workplaces good for those groups are largely the conditions that make workplaces good in general. In their study of over 800 companies, the authors found that straightforward and relatively low-cost measures like thoughtful recruitment initiatives, formal mentorship opportunities, and work-life balance policies did more to increase workplace diversity and improve the retention of women and employees of color than the most cutting-edge antiracism trainings. "Some management practices that people don't think of as diversity measures at all are remarkably effective at opening opportunity to groups that have been shut out," they wrote.[58]

These practices also happen not to require a multibillion-dollar DEI apparatus, which must come as a disappointment to an industry whose consultants routinely charge between $100 and $500 per hour (and whose superstars can command up to $50,000 per speaking engagement). Luckily for the industry, however, one of its greatest strengths has been its ability to manufacture new reasons for its continued existence. The history and evolution of workplace race relations management since the 1964 Civil Rights Act—from equal opportunity compliance to diversity as a free market salve to racial equity as a stakeholder capitalist imperative—demonstrates the ease with which this type of human resources management has adroitly refashioned itself again and again.

In recent years, as the shortcomings of DEI have come under scrutiny from progressives and conservatives alike, industry professionals have worked to spin these failures into fresh opportunities for yet more programs. New boutique DEI consultancies sprout every year, claiming that their proprietary methods can succeed where the others have foundered; management consultants and DEI officers proffer new guides and terminologies just as the old ones start to ring hollow or fall out of fashion. In 2023, the *New York Times* reported that companies taking stock of failed or lackluster DEI initiatives were increasingly turning to an updated paradigm: diversity, equity, inclusion, and *belonging,* or DEIB.[59] ("The question of belonging has become the latest focus in the evolving world of corporate diversity, equity and inclusion programming," the paper stated.) And even the Supreme Court's overturning of affirmative action in higher education that year spurred a new wave of DEI services as law firms anticipated increased hostility from Republicans and future court battles over the issue. "As long as businesses are interested in doing diversity, equity and inclusion, they are going to need legal advice," one management lawyer told *Bloomberg Law.*[60]

Meanwhile, progressives—perhaps inadvertently—have continued to encourage the further expansion of the industry by arguing that past DEI measures have been ineffective only because employers and the industry itself haven't been committed to a sufficiently radical vision of antiracism. "While many recent studies raise legitimate concerns about diversity practices, most have overshadowed the extent to which these initiatives ceased to be seen as a moral imperative linked to centuries of systemic racial oppression," journalism professor Pamela Newkirk has written.[61] DEI consultant Kim Tran has similarly argued, "The multibillion-dollar juggernaut has left its social justice principles, and the people who established them, far behind. DEI needs to shed its bourgeois skin."[62]

But given the industry's very genesis in private-sector human resources management, the bourgeois character of contemporary DEI arguably runs much deeper than its exterior. And the project of bringing DEI into closer alignment with activist sensibilities not only facilitates the industry's continual cycle of renewal and rebirth but conveniently supplies moral justification for each new wave of DEI initiatives and the growth of more for-profit DEI enterprises. For instance, in the wake of 2020's reckoning, a group of corporate executives partnered with nonprofits to establish the Corporate Racial Equity Alliance, a new organization dedicated to building "antiracist, equitable corporations." Sounding very much like the progressive critics of DEI, the group noted that token measures—"an implicit bias training, or hiring that one Black person on their board, or issuing a public statement in support of Black Lives Matter"—had failed to transform American corporations.[63] In a nod to the bestselling *How to Be Antiracist*—which famously posits that there's no way to be non-racist, only racist or steadfastly antiracist—the group urged CEOs to "design HR policies and practices that are actively antiracist, not merely 'not racist.'" That same year, a *Harvard Business Review* author exhorted businesses to move "beyond diversity" to the more substantive goal of racial equity.[64] "It's clear that the suite of diversity and inclusion tools and practices that went mainstream in the '90s are grossly insufficient for racial equity work," he wrote, before recommending programs like mandatory "multi-day anti-racism trainings" for staffers.

Business leaders, in other words, have found numerous ways to use activist antiracist frameworks to their advantage. At the more specialized end of the labor market, where job applicants must present an ever-expanding list of credentials, fluency in the most up-to-date antiracism has become another way for managers to screen and select potential employees. This is especially true of hypercompetitive fields like academia, where tenure-track positions are vanishing and a single job posting can attract hundreds of qualified applicants. By one estimate, up to a third of American universities and colleges today require faculty candidates to submit DEI statements, or documents that detail the applicant's personal commitment to (and accomplishments regarding) racial justice in their work, thereby demonstrating their familiarity with—if not fealty to— the most current language and standards of DEI. Though the use of these statements has generated controversy and a handful of prominent institutions including MIT and Harvard have scrapped them in recent years, they remain a central component of hiring within the University of California system and other large universities. The use of DEI as a job qualification has also spread to parts of the corporate world. A 2021 job listing for a store director position at Target, for instance, stated that a successful candidate would "demonstrate a commitment to diversity, equity, and inclusion through continuous development, modeling inclusive behaviors, and proactively managing bias." And guru Robin DiAngelo has insisted that mastering the rites of DEI in the twenty-first century is so important that those not up to the task might as well not hold jobs at all. "We have to see the ability to engage in these conversations with some nuance and some skill as a basic qualification, and if you can't do that, you're just simply not qualified in today's workplace," she said at a 2023 panel discussion.[65]

It's hardly surprising, then, that universities have constructed entire programs around this skillset. In addition to the DEI certificates or special concentrations that are currently available from dozens of colleges, Bentley University offers an entire undergraduate program in DEI, while students at Tufts University can obtain a master's degree in Diversity, Equity, Inclusion, and Justice Leadership. In 2023, the prestigious Wharton business school at the University of Pennsylvania officially debuted two new majors to address "two burgeoning industry priorities": DEI and ESGB, or Environmental, Social and Governance Factors for Business.[66]

Though racial justice advocates and the business press alike had speculated that private-sector DEI might be on the chopping block after the Supreme Court's 2023 ruling striking down affirmative action in higher education, one 2024 survey conducted by the employer-side law firm Littler Mendelson found that 91 percent of executives had continued to prioritize DEI after the ruling and most had even expanded their programs.[67] Today, despite various right-wing efforts to eliminate DEI programs—and a handful of corporate defections as a result of that pressure—the practice continues to flourish. "People may not be jumping up and down and screaming 'DEI' from the rooftops, but the work continues," one management consultant told the *Financial Times* in 2024.[68] Just as the corporate sector had responded to Reagan's assault on affirmative action in the '80s by expanding—rather than cutting—their internal diversity practices, most business leaders today have signaled a commitment to continue DEI, though perhaps under a new set of names. "In the 60-plus conversations I had with leaders in attendance at Davos, there was an intentionality about racial equity that was palpable," the executive director of the W.K. Kellogg Foundation wrote in 2024.

In fact, in the aftermath of the Supreme Court's ruling on affirmative action the year before, major corporations had already publicly reaffirmed such commitments.[69] "Regardless of this week's Supreme Court decisions, I want you to know that our commitment to building an inclusive and diverse Starbucks remains stronger than ever," Sara Kelly, Starbucks's executive vice president said in an HR dispatch to employees.[70] For years, Starbucks had cultivated a reputation as a celebrated progressive employer through HR policies such as companywide anti-racism training, careful attention to eliminating pay disparities by race or gender, and offering transgender health care in its benefits package. "We will continue to pursue programs and policies to foster inclusion for our partners, customers and communities," Kelly promised. It was, incidentally, also the same year that a National Labor Relations Board judge determined that the company had committed hundreds of violations of labor law in a nationwide offensive to quash employees' efforts to unionize.

3
CLASS DISMISSED

When the dust had settled after 2020's volatile summer of street demonstrations, it was difficult to determine what—if anything—had changed in the way of policing or criminal justice reform in the country. In the immediate wake of the protests, some municipalities had passed piecemeal measures like chokehold bans or experimented with dispatching unarmed non-police responders to mental health emergencies. But by the next year, a more comprehensive federal bill on policing reform died in Congress. "A year after the death of George Floyd, many Americans routinely describe the protests that followed last summer as a singular, racially transformative moment," CNN commentator John Blake wrote in May of 2021.[1] "But I've reached an uncomfortable conclusion: Floyd's death did not lead to a racial reckoning."

Over the next several years, even as police killings in the US increased slightly rather than abated, crime spikes in large cities effectively extinguished any mass appetite for major overhauls to the criminal justice system, let alone defunding or shrinking the size of police forces. Faced with officer shortages and rising rates of murder and gun violence, liberal cities that had pledged to cut or reallocate police budgets at the height of the demonstrations—Los Angeles; Burlington, Vermont; and Portland, Oregon; among others—sheepishly restored and even *increased* police spending, while voters in Minneapolis, home of George Floyd and ground zero for the 2020 demonstrations, decisively rejected a ballot measure to dismantle the police department. By the start of 2023, even widely reported police killings—for instance, the brutal beating of Tyre Nichols by police officers in Memphis or the LAPD's tasering of Keenan Anderson, a cousin of prominent Black Lives Matter activist Patrisse Cullors—would draw only a thin shadow of the protests that had engulfed 2020.

As the momentum to transform policing in the US fizzled, so did public support for Black Lives Matter. Less than year after NPR had launched a special series commemorating the "Summer of Racial Reckoning," the network's Code Switch show ran a segment titled "The Racial Reckoning That Wasn't."[2] According to program guests Jennifer Chudy and Hakeem Jefferson, two researchers studying shifts in public opinion on the protests, support for Black Lives Matter among Americans had been fleeting, surging to record highs in the immediate weeks following Floyd's death, then falling steeply over the subsequent months. By the next year, public support for Black Lives Matter was even lower than it had been prior to the 2020 protests, particularly among Republicans and white respondents. Ultimately, the researchers concluded, only a small minority of whites had continued to "care about anti-black racism" throughout the changing tides of public sentiment. "They are a tiny, tiny, tiny, tiny, tiny percentage of the population," Chudy said.

There was, however, still a contingent committed to carrying the torch even after the protests had subsided and public opinion had dwindled. That fall, just as support for Black Lives Matter among the general public reached a nadir, the MacArthur Foundation awarded one of its coveted "genius grants" of $625,000 to Ibram Kendi for his writing on race. Just a few months later, another major philanthropic donor, the Mellon Foundation, announced $72 million in funding for new racial justice projects in the humanities. And NPR listeners, too, had remained steadfast in their antiracism: "Here on Code Switch, we're always hearing from white people who write in and talk to us about all the reasons why they want to be antiracist and how hard they're working on that," host Shereen Marisol Meraji said. "So I want to know, who are those white people who make up that tiny percentage who are sympathetic?"

"You know, they do tend to live in cities," Chudy replied thoughtfully. "I should say the other kind of reliable predictor is that they tend to have higher levels of education."

Managers of the Antiracist Order

Despite little policing reform and a widespread sense of disappointment among racial justice activists and liberal media commentators in the years after the Floyd protests, a racial reckoning *had* taken place the summer of 2020 and had, moreover, been a resounding success in at least one notable way.

Though people from all walks of life had participated in 2020's demonstrations, that year it was the affluent and their institutions that generated and sustained the national *reckoning,* understood as both an exhaustive accounting of past and present racial injustice in the US and also a moment of judgment that demanded a decisive sorting of the racists from the antiracists. In knowledge work and creative fields like the media, academia, the arts, and philanthropy, college-educated professionals waged a sweeping campaign of antiracist consciousness-raising that extended well after the summer and arguably continues in some form today. The immediate effect of this protracted reckoning—which insisted that racism was a structural force and race the most consequential division in America—was to displace the question of class while simultaneously securing for professionals their historical role as enlightened brokers of the social order.

Though 2020's protests had commenced in the name of George Floyd—a working-class Twin Cities resident who had lived in public housing as a child; dropped out of community college; and worked mainly manual and service jobs, including the restaurant gig from which he had been laid off during the pandemic—the instigators and most faithful adherents of the national soul-searching that quickly mushroomed around the demonstrations were largely members of what the writers Barbara Ehrenreich and John Ehrenreich called the professional-managerial class.[3] The PMC, the Ehrenreichs wrote in 1977, was the credentialed, white-collar stratum between capital and labor. While its members worked for a living like the traditional working class, they earned salaries rather than hourly wages and enjoyed a degree of autonomy, authority, and status denied to their blue-collar counterparts. Most crucially, the PMC's intermediate position in the capitalist hierarchy granted its members a pivotal role in molding and maintaining the economic order. Starting in the nineteenth century, professionals had pioneered both overt and indirect forms of worker control, from workplace "scientific management" techniques designed to wring greater productivity from the toiling masses to the propaganda—art, literature, and entertainment—that ran ideological cover for capitalists. "Almost every profession or would-be profession, from sociology to home economics, had something to offer in the great task of 'taming' the American working class," Barbara Ehrenreich observed in her 1989 book *Fear of Falling*.[4]

But if the PMC had frequently served both willingly and inadvertently as henchmen of the ruling class, their peculiar middleman role in the order also meant that their relationship to capital was prone to its own kind of antagonism. Vulnerable themselves to attacks from above on their professions and paychecks, the PMC had also functioned on occasion as "a 'liberal' force, defending the values of scholarship and human service in the face of the relentless pursuit of profit."[5] This tension, the Ehrenreichs argued in a 2013 update to their original essay, only grew more pronounced in the throes of neoliberalism, as it became increasingly apparent that automation, job outsourcing, and attacks on labor—or the same conditions that blue-collar workers had weathered for decades—had finally come for the PMC, too.

While the twenty-first-century economy had boosted a handful of professionals into a tier of exorbitantly wealthy CEOs and supermanagers, it had also had the effect of eroding numerous white-collar professions. Newspaper journalism had suffered a catastrophic decline, and universities were steadily bleeding tenure-track jobs. Though more Americans than ever before held college degrees in the new millennium, the value of those degrees had slipped precipitously. By the eve of the Great Recession, skyrocketing tuition costs had generated nearly a trillion dollars of student debt and pushed a growing number of middle-class families toward financial insolvency. The downwardly mobile members of the contemporary PMC, the Ehrenreichs argued, therefore had a choice before them: They could join with the traditional working class to fight against capital or resign themselves to demise. "In the coming years, we expect to see the remnants of the PMC increasingly making common cause with the remnants of the traditional working class for, at a minimum, representation in the political process," they concluded.[6]

That decade, a number of would-be members of the PMC indeed saw themselves as part of an exploited majority, or the 99 percent, as the Occupy Wall Street slogan went. The millennial cohort that had graduated into the recession with college degrees yet dim economic prospects not only powered Occupy encampments and marches across the country but boosted Bernie Sanders to a surprising string of wins during the 2016 Democratic primary just a few years later. Disillusioned grads also flocked to explicitly anticapitalist organizations like the Democratic Socialists of America, whose membership grew from a sclerotic 5,000 just prior to Sanders's run to more than 66,000 by 2020.[7]

But if nearly half a century of neoliberalism had demoted some of the PMC to proletarians, it had also turbocharged the credentials arms race within the very professions that it was dissolving. The steady contraction of jobs in prestige sectors like media, the arts, and academia has meant that competition for the shrinking number of positions within them is fierce, and the fields themselves even more rarified as a result. Journalism, for example, is now the near-exclusive domain of the rich thanks to the disappearance of the kinds of local newspapers and alt weeklies that had once provided young people from a variety of backgrounds with entry-level reporting jobs. The outlets flush enough to have survived the gutting of the industry—mostly glossy corporate magazines and national papers like the *New York Times* and the *Wall Street Journal*—disproportionately draw their staffers from Ivy League universities and other private colleges.[8] "Ironically, even as the economic fortunes of the news media have declined precipitously, as a social group the status of journalists has increased," media studies professor Daniel Kreiss wrote in 2018.[9]

Furthermore, while the Great Recession had evinced the enormous chasm between the 1 percent and everyone else, the economic downturn triggered by the 2020 Covid pandemic sharpened the fault line between mental and manual workers. Though it was, as before, the ultrarich that reaped the greatest windfalls that year, a palpable division widened between the white-collar professionals able to work remotely—many of whom spent their lockdowns baking bread, decamping to countryside rentals, or setting up "schooling pods" for their children with other affluent parents—and the warehouse workers, nursing home staffers, mail carriers, and other frontline workers, who kept the economy afloat at risk to their own health, and the service sector employees who suffered mass layoffs from business closures.

According to an analysis by the *Washington Post*, the upper-middle class—that is, the top 20 to 25 percent of income earners—quickly found their feet during the Covid recession even as financial hardship for workers making less than $20 an hour continued to mount.[10] "By the end of the summer, the downturn was largely over for the wealthy—white-collar jobs had mostly rebounded, along with home values and stock prices," the *Post* noted. "The shift to remote work strongly favored more-educated workers, with as many as 6 in 10 college-educated employees working from home at the outset of the crisis, compared with about 1 in 7 who have only high school diplomas." The next year, the recovery was still uneven enough that economists had begun calling it "K-shaped" to describe the conspicuous divergence of fortunes between workers with college degrees and those without; unemployment rates for the latter group remained distressingly high through the fall of 2021.

America's white-collar workforce, in other words, had passed the pandemic in a position of relative stability even in the midst of a wider economic upheaval. But it was also the fourth year of a tumultuous Trump presidency in which the same group of liberal professionals had fought fiercely to reclaim their role as a civilizing force in society, rallying to defend institutions like the media, the Supreme Court, and even the FBI against Trump's erratic attacks. The Trump administration's belated and haphazard Covid response further inflamed partisan divides and spawned a fresh round of appeals to expertise and science by Democrats, who anointed figures like Center for Disease Control director Anthony Fauci and New York's then-governor Andrew Cuomo as voices of reason, professionalism, and objectivity against a reckless Trump regime.

Floyd's death in 2020—which came not only on the heels of several other brutal killings of black Americans, but also at the height of widespread apprehension over what was then a pandemic spiraling out of control—galvanized anxious liberals around a shared project of radical social overhaul. That year, however, the PMC's desire to remake society manifested not as a movement for broad public investment or a stand against the rapacious corporate sector and billionaires that had profited from the volatility of the pandemic but instead as a mission to construct a consciously antiracist society through a transformation of the country's richest and most powerful cultural institutions.

In the cash-flush art world, museums and galleries announced new DEI programs and commitments to hiring more black leaders or acquiring works by black artists.[11] The Metropolitan Museum of Art, for instance, pledged $10 million to "increase the amount of works by BIPOC artists" in its collections while blue-chip gallery owner David Zwirner commissioned the opening of a new Manhattan gallery to be run by an all-black staff. The nation's leading media outlets and publishers likewise threw themselves into the project of racial justice, rushing out special issues and permanent verticals dedicated to illuminating the legacy of racism in America. The *Boston Globe* appointed Kendi to oversee a brand new digital magazine on race with a seven-figure budget just as staffers alleged racially insensitive work environments and demanded new, diverse leadership at other influential publications, from women's media like *Vogue* and Refinery29 to the food magazine *Bon Appetit* to the public radio station WNYC.[12] An uproar over the *New York Times'* decision to publish an op-ed by senator Tom Cotton calling for military suppression of rioting led to the swift ouster of a longtime editor from the paper while the *Philadelphia Inquirer* came under fire for running an opinion piece critical of the rioting titled "Buildings matter, too" (and subsequently commissioned Temple University's journalism department to conduct a year-long audit of its race coverage as an apology.)[13] "The fallout in the media world has been faster and more extensive than the impact of the #MeToo movement in 2017 and 2018," the *Washington Post* noted after a whirlwind nine days in June 2020 in which five editors at top publications departed following reckoning-related scandals.[14]

Among America's educational institutions, the energy of the soul-searching seemed to rise in direct proportion to the cost and prestige of the school in question. At the New York prep school Dalton, where annual tuition exceeds $55,000, more than 120 faculty members, students, and alumni signed a petition calling on the school to implement new antiracism measures, including required coursework on "Black liberation," mandatory annual antiracism training for all staffers and parent volunteers, and the appointment of no fewer than a dozen full-time DEI officers.[15] Hundreds of universities that had temporarily stopped requiring standardized test scores from applicants during the pandemic—Ivy League schools and the entire University of California system, among others— announced they would permanently cease using such tests in their applications processes in order to boost the racial diversity of incoming classes.[16] Selective K–12 schools in large coastal cities also moved to stop or reduce standardized testing on racial equity grounds; in a 2020 testimony urging the Boston school board to eliminate such testing, Kendi himself stated, "Standardized tests have become the most effective racist weapon ever devised to objectively degrade Black and Brown minds and legally exclude their bodies from prestigious schools."[17] By 2022, to much media fanfare, Harvard University would release a comprehensive report detailing the university's historical ties to slavery and announce the creation of a $100 million fund to explore the issue of reparations.[18]

Against the backdrop of mass protests, the most prominent and powerful cultural institutions in the US promised that they were finally doing the work; they would dismantle structural racism and antiblackness, decolonize reading lists and museum exhibits, and confront white supremacy within their own ranks. That summer, the antiracist fervor reached even the most insulated and famously out-of-touch layer of the culture industry as a wave of A-list celebrities joined street marches (Ariana Grande, Ben Affleck) or donated lavishly to bail funds and racial justice charities (Chrissy Teigen, Kanye West). Selena Gomez turned over her Instagram account, followed at the time by nearly 180 million people, to Kendi and Black Lives Matter cofounder Alicia Garza; Harry Styles delivered a primer on white privilege via his social media feeds. "I do things every day without fear, because I am privileged, and I am privileged every day because I am white," he wrote.[19] "Being not racist is not enough, we must be anti racist."

Though there was no reason to believe that this outpouring was anything other than earnest, it was also a type of politics that would fundamentally legitimize a professional-class vision of justice and reaffirm the PMC's role as stewards of that system. The reckoning was an expression of the collective anxieties of a twenty-first-century PMC that was itself drifting toward precarity and scrambling to hold fast to its dwindling advantages. Antiracism, or the commitment to eliminating racial disparities from American life—by any means necessary, for those inclined to its most militant version—was a framework that allowed professionals to agitate for the radical demographic reorganization of their institutions while simultaneously reaffirming the authority and elite status of those institutions within a capitalist hierarchy. And within the prestigious fields that had undergone the most tumultuous personnel upheavals in 2020, broadcasting one's position at the vanguard of antiracism was a way to demonstrate that one was qualified to be a member of the enlightened professions, particularly at a time when plum positions within so many of those professions were steadily vanishing.

The Ehrenreichs had observed a similar dynamic among the middle-class New Left radicals of the '60s and '70s, whose dreams of revolution conveniently tended to preserve their own capacity as experts and administrators of the post-revolutionary society. "PMC radicalism emerged out of PMC class interests, which include the PMC's interest in extending its cultural and technological hegemony over the working class," they wrote.[20] "Thus the possibility exists in the PMC for the emergence of what may at first seem to be a contradiction in terms: anti-working class radicalism."

Life and Death in the Twenty-First Century

In 1997 the sociologist Eduardo Bonilla-Silva argued that while racism in the US had mutated throughout history—evolving from the overt domination of chattel slavery and Jim Crow to subtler or less visible forms of oppression in the post–Civil Rights era—one factor had remained constant over time. "The unchanging element throughout these stages is that Blacks' life chances are significantly lower than those of Whites, and ultimately a racialized social order is distinguished by this difference in life chances," he wrote in a paper that would become one of the foundational texts of the concept of structural racism.[21]

In the nearly three decades since Bonilla-Silva's writing, however, this understanding of racism has been complicated by the fact that class stratification has sharpened so dramatically *within* racial groups that race itself is an increasingly imprecise determinant of a given person's life chances. A 2022 study by researchers Anne Case and Angus Deaton confirmed that people without a college degree within every racial group were dying much faster than those with one.[22] At the same time, they noted, the gaps *between* blacks and whites were starting to close. Between 1990 and 2018, the black-white life expectancy gap had closed by more than 50 percent according to one estimate.[23] "As educational gaps have widened, racial gaps have narrowed, so that blacks with a BA are now closer to whites with a BA than they are to blacks without a BA, the opposite of the situation in 1992 and up to around 2000," Case and Deaton wrote. Just a few years earlier, an analysis by the *Washington Post* had similarly shown that in at least thirty rural counties in the South, mortality rates for middle-aged white women had surpassed those of black women of the same age bracket, a set of circumstances that had been unthinkable twenty years ago.[24]

In other words, in the twenty-first century, any material security that may have once been associated with "whiteness" has all but vanished for whites without a college degree, which functions as a proxy (if an often crude one) for class. Throughout the previous century, the life chances of well-off black people had been much more comparable to the life chances of poor black people than to the life chances of whites of their own socioeconomic level. Today, however, whites and blacks without college degrees have much more similar life chances to each other than they do to college graduates of their own racial group, which is, in a way, a gruesome kind of racial equity at work.

One reason for the convergence is that starting around 2010, premature deaths from drug overdoses, alcohol-related diseases, and suicide—what Case and Deaton have called "deaths of despair"—have risen precipitously among whites with a high school education or less. In 2017 alone, Case and

Deaton observed, there were around 158,000 fatalities of this kind in the US, or "the equivalent of three fully loaded Boeing 737 MAX jets falling out of the sky every day for a year."[25] Thanks to these and other health inequalities—particularly rising rates of cardiovascular disease among lower-income Americans—the less fortunate are now dying so prematurely that it's dragged down the average life expectancy in the US, which is now lower than that of other rich nations, and even lower than that of several much poorer ones, including Cuba and Lebanon.[26] Probably to the surprise of no one, affluent Americans have been spared from this trend; by 2021, the average life expectancy for an American with a college degree was around eight and half years longer than for those without one.[27]

Present day economic inequality also complicates the picture of the black-white racial wealth gap, another metric frequently invoked to demonstrate the stark material divide between blacks and whites. On paper, the median white household in the US owns about $189,000 in assets, whereas the median black household owns only $24,000.[28] An even more dire picture emerges when one examines the average (or mean) wealth of white households compared to the average wealth of black households; by this measure, average white household wealth is around $840,000 greater than the average black household wealth. "Perhaps no statistic better illustrates the enduring legacy of our country's shameful history of treating black people as sub-citizens, sub-Americans, and sub-humans than the wealth gap," author Ta-Nehisi Coates has written.[29]

But sobering as these figures are, the fixation on the black-white wealth gap also conceals the enormous (and still growing) inequality *within* racial groups. The think tank People's Policy Project has shown that nearly 78 percent of the current black-white racial wealth gap is driven by the richest 10 percent of each racial group, which is, after all, the bracket that holds most of the wealth in our contemporary gilded age.[30] To put it another way, the racial wealth gap looks as stark as it does mostly because of the extreme wealth of a small number of rich whites. But this also means that closing most of the existing wealth gap between blacks and whites—*without first closing the massive wealth gap between the rich and the poor*—would largely necessitate making already-rich black people richer, while conversely, very little of the racial wealth gap would be closed by helping poor black people acquire more wealth, since the bottom 50 percent of both blacks *and* whites own almost no wealth at all.

Likewise, even as activists and commentators have insisted upon racism as the primary driver of police violence and mass incarceration—the "New Jim Crow," as law professor Michelle Alexander has famously characterized it—the shifting demographics of the prison population over the last two decades suggest a somewhat different explanation. Since 2000, the black incarceration rate has fallen by about 22 percent while the incarceration rate for whites has increased by more than 40 percent.[31] Of course, blacks, at around 13 percent of the US population, are still drastically overrepresented in the prison system, where they make up about 33 percent of inmates. But even though it's clear that racism continues to permeate the criminal justice system, it's also the case that the majority of people in prison (and the majority of people killed by the police) *aren't* black; in fact, the far more common denominator among those who end up behind bars is class. Today, for instance, a black college graduate is several percentage points more likely to end up in prison than a white college grad but fifteen times *less* likely to be incarcerated than whites with only a high school education. "The evidence should make plain that poor whites and Hispanics are not really collateral damage in a war on black people that goes back to slavery and emancipation's unfulfilled promise," historian Touré Reed has noted.[32] "I think it might be more accurate to say that middle-class black people and upper-class black people are occasionally collateral damage in a war on poor people."

The point, to be perfectly clear, isn't that racism has vanished or that poor whites now somehow have it worse than blacks (as a few critics of Case and Deaton have suggested they've claimed).[33] The point is rather that extreme economic inequality has cleaved *every* racial category so dramatically over the last two decades that the notion of collective racial advantages and disadvantages obfuscates more than it reveals. Even a popular antiracist concept like "white privilege" unravels on all but the most abstract level when you consider that this privilege is somehow supposed to extend in equal measure to, say, British multimillionaire Harry Styles *and* the whites with zero or negative wealth who work for poverty wages or find themselves in the crosshairs of the police.

Writing Off Economic Anxiety

Over the same period that the economic stability of the entire working class cratered, the PMC's preoccupation with race inflated to colossal proportions. Even prior to 2020's reckoning, liberal academics, media commentators, and progressive NGOs and think tanks had already collectively embraced the project of "taxonomizing apparent racial disparities as instances of the workings of trans-historical racism or white supremacy," as political scientist Adolph Reed Jr. has put it.[34] Soon after the first Black Lives Matter protests erupted in 2013, for instance, the Democracy Alliance—a coalition of exceptionally rich donors including billionaires George Soros and Tom Steyer—convened a summit on the provision of long-term funding to racial justice groups.[35] And by 2020, even the most rarefied, elite secret societies at Ivy League universities were explicitly committed to racial equity. According to the *Atlantic*, Yale University's exclusive Skull and Bones society—famous for incubating former president George W. Bush and various other masters of the universe—had undertaken drastic measures to diversify its ranks and admitted its first entirely non-white class that year.

Though this isn't a conspiracy, it's also not a coincidence. Among other functions, the zeal for identifying and decrying extant racial disparities, which reached a fever pitch during the Trump presidency and 2020's racial reckoning, has allowed those who still occupy relatively comfortable perches in the economic order to justify both their status and the order itself by recasting a number of the symptoms of working-class

discontent as nothing more than outbursts of racial resentment harbored by downscale whites.

This sentiment manifested most notably after Trump's
surprise victory in the 2016 election, which renewed a liberal
contempt for the working class behind the veneer of racial
sensitivity. When a few public figures attempted to address the
economic and political conditions that had seeded the ground
for Trump's win, they were roundly excoriated by the same
media that had assured audiences of a Clinton presidency.
Bernie Sanders, for instance, came under fire for suggesting that
the Democrats' electoral losses that year were perhaps at least
partly the fault of the party itself, not simply a sign of a hope-
lessly bigoted electorate. "I think there needs to be a profound
change in the way the Democratic Party does business," he
said in a CBS interview.[36] "I come from the white working
class, and I am deeply humiliated that the Democratic Party
cannot talk to the people where I came from." Soon after this
appearance, Ta-Nehisi Coates characterized Sanders's remarks
as "a sweeping dismissal of the concerns of those who don't
share kinship with white men," and the idea that "economic
anxiety" was a cheap excuse meant only to conceal the seething
racism of Trump voters quickly became the consensus among
the liberal commentariat.[37]

Piece after piece insisted, "Top Democrats Are Wrong:
Trump Supporters Were More Motivated by Racism Than
Economic Issues" (the *Intercept*), "It Was Cultural Anxiety
That Drove White, Working-Class Voters to Trump" (the
Atlantic), "Trump Voters Driven by Fear of Losing Status,
Not Economic Anxiety, Study Finds," (the *New York Times*),

and "White Fear Elected Trump" (*Salon*). "This is not, in fact, about economic anxiety," the economist Paul Krugman announced on CNN.[38] "Ultimately, it's about race. You cannot understand anything that's happening in this election or in US politics without seeing it as a certain, unfortunately large, fraction of Americans who don't like the fact that we're becoming a multiracial, multicultural country." He added with a slight smirk, "Among people I talk to, 'economic anxiety' has become kind of a joke slogan." Media insiders continued to scoff at the joke slogan well into the Trump presidency; in a 2018 column, journalist and MSNBC host Mehdi Hasan proclaimed economic anxiety a "complete and utter myth" and a "zombie argument" that had been "shot down repeatedly by the experts over the past 18 months."[39] Citing several studies documenting the racial resentments of Trump voters, he demanded, "How can this still be a matter for debate?"

But despite Hasan's and other commentators' insistence that experts had conclusively settled the question of what had driven voters to Trump, there was also plenty of evidence that pointed to a different explanation for Trump's appeal among certain sections of the voting public that year. None of it, however, had managed to capture the attention of the media quite like the notion of a reactionary white working class lashing out after two terms of the country's first black president.

After nearly every election, it's become routine for political commentators to lament that working-class voters who cast ballots for Republicans—a party that is, after all, hostile to unions and uniformly committed to destroying the social safety net—are "voting against their interests." But in certain parts of the US, working-class votes for Republicans can also be understood as votes *against* the party that claimed to represent their interests and then left them by the wayside. This is part of the long-reaching legacy of deindustrialization, a process that was kickstarted in the latter half of the twentieth century as the corporate sector increasingly turned to offshoring to cut labor costs and break unions. The economic crash of the 1970s and a series of capital-friendly trade policies enacted over the next several decades decimated America's manufacturing sector, gutting a once robust steel industry and setting the US on the path to a massive trade deficit. According to the economist Barry Bluestone, widespread closures of steel plants and other factories during the '70s and '80s ultimately cost an estimated 32 million jobs.[40]

The mania for free trade among the bipartisan political establishment only spread from there. While it was Ronald Reagan and his successor George H. W. Bush who began the push for a North American free trade zone, the dream was cemented into law by Democratic president Bill Clinton in 1993 as the North American Free Trade Agreement (NAFTA). NAFTA struck down tariffs and regulations deemed to interfere with trade between the US and other North American countries, thereby granting corporations new leeway not only to accelerate the outsourcing of jobs to places where they could pay workers far less than the US minimum wage but also to skirt various environmental and public health protections. Over the next decade, free trade enriched corporations and their shareholders while simultaneously laying waste to an already struggling manufacturing sector. In 2014, on the twentieth anniversary of NAFTA's implementation, the Economic Policy Institute estimated that the deal had cost nearly 700,000 American jobs.[41] "NAFTA granted corporations extraordinary legal protections against national labor and environmental laws that they could claim threatened future profits," EPI founder Jeff Faux wrote. "At the same time, workers and unions were denied the legal status needed to defend themselves in these new cross-border jurisdictions."

It was all but inevitable, then, that in the aftermath of NAFTA, some voters would sour on the party that had hastened the end of some of the last good jobs for workers with only a high school education. One 2021 study found that white voters without college degrees in several historically Democratic counties that had shed manufacturing jobs in the 1990s were solidly casting ballots for Republicans by the year 2000.[42] "Voters in the places most impacted by NAFTA and voters who oppose free trade left the Democratic party in large numbers beginning around the time of NAFTA's debate and implementation," the authors observed.

Another report published that year offered a sobering assessment of the crumbling of the electoral "Blue Wall," a string of once-reliable Democratic counties in America's industrial heartland that had flipped red in 2016. In an analysis of voting patterns in midsize factory towns across ten Rust Belt states, Democratic strategist Richard Martin found that although Barack Obama had handily won such towns in 2008—and then again by more than 100,000 votes in 2012—Hillary Clinton would go on to lose the very same areas by more than 800,000 votes.[43] Her name, it seemed, was a greater liability in this region than the former president's skin color. "In Donald Trump's first debate with Hillary Clinton, he mentioned 'unfair' trade deals 9 times, NAFTA 8 times, and kept reminding people it was Hillary's husband who signed it," Martin observed. That year, CNN noted with some amusement that Trump's campaign speeches on trade sounded nearly identical to Bernie Sanders's, a politician who had fiercely opposed NAFTA in Congress in the '90s, and the only other presidential candidate in 2016 who had openly discussed the effects of free trade on American jobs and the working class.[44] Trump's rhetoric on trade was a departure not only from the other GOP candidates that year but also from a Democratic Party increasingly associated with Silicon Valley, selective universities, and expensive coastal metropoles. "Trump took the Bernie-style populism, emptied it of real class politics, reduced it to a jumble of affective associations, and used it to beat-up the smug liberals of the professional managerial class," journalist Christian Parenti wrote of the tactic.[45] "It worked."

Former manufacturing workers in hollowed-out blue-collar towns across the US would themselves say the same. In the wake of the election, sociologist Andrew Cherlin conducted a series of in-depth interviews with residents of Dundalk, Maryland, a former steel town a few miles outside of Baltimore. That year, a number of residents had welcomed Trump's calls for steel tariffs and other protectionist talking points on trade even as they questioned the depth of his sincerity; 66 percent went on to cast votes for him. "I'll be honest with you, I'm not sure if what the guy is doing with regard to China or with regard to GM is actually going to work," one former factory worker told Cherlin. "But it does on a certain level thrill me that someone is actually doing something and at least treating this like it's an issue, rather than just a thing we have to accept."[46]

Like other factory towns, Dundalk had undergone a decades-long decline from its peak as a thriving manufacturing hub in the postwar period. In 1960, though 70 percent of the town's adult residents hadn't graduated from high school, Dundalk's median household income was well over the national average and the majority of families owned their homes, thanks to high-paying union jobs at nearby manufacturing plants like General Motors, Western Electric, and, most crucially, the Bethlehem Steel Company. This standard of living, however, began to slip away in the 1970s as a recession and an influx of cheap imports devastated the steel industry. When the Bethlehem Steel plant finally closed in 2012, only 8 percent of the town's labor force was still employed in manufacturing. By that point, Dundalk's population had dwindled and opioid addiction was on the rise. According to one social worker, the majority of residents had turned to unstable and low-paid service sector or health care jobs in the absence of the factory jobs that had once sustained the town's families. "They are not livable jobs with livable pay," she told Cherlin.[47]

In 2016, Trump's populist message on industry resonated in a town not only that had suffered decades of falling wages and the permanent disappearance of a type of work that gave residents a sense of pride but that was completely invisible in the eyes of the political establishment. One Dundalk resident recalled that when he and a group of other steelworkers had gone to Washington in the early 2000s to lobby for tariffs on imported steel, neither Democrats nor Republicans had been willing to listen. It wasn't until 2016 that he would hear a presidential candidate invoke steel tariffs on a national platform.[48] The former steelworker, Cherlin noted, "took off his glasses and fought back tears as he related how it felt, many years later, to listen to the ceremony at which President Trump signed an order establishing tariffs on imported steel." Like others, he acknowledged that the tariffs weren't likely to revive the steel industry. But, he maintained, "Trump had at least acted."

Dundalk's economic backslide, it turned out, also had a way of inflaming the very cultural and racial grievances that the media had seized upon in the wake of Trump's election. Several white residents had openly expressed their woes in racial terms, complaining, for instance, about new Section 8 housing—code for low-income black families—or increased immigration at the same time that they lamented the lack of good jobs in the area. ("I think it's easy to look out and see someone who looks different than you and think they're the problem," one white former steelworker observed.[49] "Then, when that's backed up by some politician with an agenda, you feel justified.") But it was precisely the backdrop of economic hardship that had made Trump's blend of populist protectionism and racial antagonism so persuasive. "Trump's masterstroke was to recognize the desperation of the white working class over the deteriorating industrial economy and encourage their tendency to racialize that desperation and blame outsiders," Cherlin wrote.

To put it another way, when economic conditions deteriorate and thrust people into a sense of loss—if not outright immiseration—the opportunities for demagogues to stoke racial resentment are that much greater. More than seventy years earlier, the legal scholar and civil rights activist Pauli Murray had identified the pernicious relationship between economic scarcity and rising racial resentment. "When jobs are plentiful, all kinds of economic discrimination are minimized," Murray wrote in a 1945 paper on hiring discrimination.[50] "When jobs are scarce, and the competition among workers for available openings is sharpened, it is relatively easy to divide employees into convenient groups provided by the incident of race, color, or religion, and to aggravate the prejudice which leads to an exclusion of minority groups from job opportunities." This has always been part of the reason to take "economic anxiety" seriously, despite pundits' insistence that it holds no explanatory power: That anxiety tends to be a rather powerful motor for racial prejudice.

And yet another irony of the media's aggressive dismissals of the country's economic deterioration in favor of race-centered explanations was that very same process of deindustrialization that had kicked Rust Belt whites down the economic ladder had also obliterated an important source of upward mobility for black workers. In the postwar era, the explosive growth of industrial unions combined with several key pieces of anti-discrimination legislation had facilitated the entry of black workers into unionized, high-wage sectors like auto and steel, creating the foundation for a blue-collar black middle class. But the very same gutting of manufacturing that had destroyed the livelihoods of white blue-collar workers would, of course, also affect black workers in those industries in equal—and often greater—measure. While the wage gap between blacks and whites had narrowed significantly between 1940 and 1970, deindustrialization not only reversed that promising trend, but also increased economic inequality *within* the black population itself.[51]

Murray's contemporaries A. Philip Randolph and Bayard Rustin, the architects of the 1963 March on Washington for Jobs and Freedom, had already warned of such an outcome in the postwar period. In 1966, the A. Philip Randolph Institute released the Freedom Budget for All Americans, a policy agenda designed to complement and fortify the civil rights victories of the '60s with a guarantee of economic security for every US citizen. Like Murray, Randolph and Rustin understood full employment to be the linchpin to stability for all, but particularly for black Americans, who were disproportionately among the country's poor and unemployed. Civil rights legislation, they argued, was necessary but not sufficient for improving the lives of most blacks, and any gains that they had made during that era would eventually evaporate if jobs were to become scarce. Circumventing this fate required broad universal measures like a jobs guarantee, a national living wage, and robust public works programs.

Though at the time of its conception the Freedom Budget was backed by a number of civil rights groups and labor leaders, it never found sufficient champions in Congress to become law. And just as Randolph and Rustin had predicted, in the absence of a strong public sector and an abundance of good jobs, an increasing number of working-class blacks sank deeper into economic hardship over the next several decades, a predicament that neoliberal policymakers on both sides of the aisle belatedly

attempted to address through a battery of punitive and counterproductive measures like workfare and mass incarceration.

Today the Democratic elite's invocations of a phantasmic
"whitelash" or "white supremacy" to explain the rise of Trump
and other expressions of right-wing populism work to obscure
the repercussions of deindustrialization for working-class
Americans—white *and* black—and thereby allow the party
(along with its various think tank and media boosters) to bury
their own collusion in the policies that created the conditions
for right-wing populism to flourish in the first place. The
insistence on race as the primary driver of politics in 2016
has furthermore come to retroactively justify the Democrats'
deliberate abandonment of working-class voters for a more
upscale base, even as this strategy has increasingly spelled
electoral trouble for the party.

The Democrats' Demographic Dilemma

Over the last decade, Democrats—and white Democrats in
particular—have become well attuned to the ways that racism
and discrimination have limited economic opportunities for
black Americans. According to one voter survey conducted
in 2011, only around a third of Democrats at the time agreed
with the statement "Over the past few years, Black people have
gotten less than they deserve." When the survey was conducted
again in 2020, however, an astonishing 73 percent said they
agreed.[52] Similarly high percentages of Democrats that year
also agreed with the statement "Slavery and discrimination
make it difficult for Black people to work their way out of the

lower class" and, conversely, disagreed with the contention that black people could be as well off as whites if they simply "tried harder."

This heightened sensitivity among Democrats to racial discrimination, however, has coincided with party elites' resurrection of a different boogeyman, particularly as the party has grown more and more solicitous of the professional-managerial class wing of the base and more responsive to the PMC institutions that have come to exert increased influence on the party in the wake of organized labor's decline. Barbara Ehrenreich had already observed the growing disdain in the 1970s among PMC liberals toward white blue-collar workers, whom they perceived as retrograde Nixon-lovers and an affront to their own sophistication. "The working class became, for many middle-class liberals, a psychic dumping ground for such unstylish sentiments as racism, male chauvinism, and crude materialism: a rearguard population that loved white bread and hated black people," she wrote in *Fear of Falling*.[53]

This notion of working-class whites as a reactionary and irredeemable force was revived with remarkable bloodlust in the aftermath of Trump's 2016 victory. The writer and Pulitzer Prize finalist Cathy Park Hong tweeted, "No more stories about the economic woes of the white working class. They're racist. Period."[54] Celebrated essayist Frank Rich published a long piece titled "No Sympathy for the Hillbilly" in which he urged the Democratic Party to avoid concerning itself with the plight of the less fortunate constituents they had lost over time.[55] "Let Trump's white working-class base take responsibility for its own votes—or in some cases failure to vote—and live with the election's consequences," he wrote. Others simply transposed onto low-income whites the same "culture of poverty" explanations that the right had been using to disparage low-income blacks for decades. "I don't see them as once proud workers, now dispossessed, but rather as people of limited ambition who might have sought better opportunity elsewhere and did not," political scientist James Stimson told the *New York Times*.[56] "I see their social problems more as explanations of why they didn't seek out opportunity when they might have than as the result of lost employment." The specter of a white working class stubbornly attached to the past and simmering in racial resentment had allowed liberals to craft a Trump-era explanation for who deserved a hand up in a deeply unequal economy and who, on the other hand, was responsible for their own hardship.

There's some evidence that liberals who embrace the concept of "white privilege" end up feeling less empathy toward poor whites relative to their empathy for poor blacks. In one recent study, researchers asked a variety of respondents to read a short passage on white privilege and found that those who held liberal views on political issues such as abortion, guns, and LGBTQ rights were *less* sympathetic to the plight of poor whites after completing the reading.[57] (The text on white privilege, as it happened, didn't much affect conservatives, who remained unsympathetic to poor whites both before *and* after the reading.) "Social liberals who think about white privilege may become more likely to blame poor white people for their poverty," the authors noted.

Especially at a time of heightened attention to race, this

perhaps explains some progressives' venom for working-class whites. But the eagerness to exchange at least part of the working class for a professional-class constituency has been a pet project of Democratic leaders since the Clinton era, when the New Democrats—the ruthless, business-savvy alliance that reoriented the party toward policies like financial deregulation and public-private partnerships—aggressively courted affluent, white-collar voters while also making plain they considered organized labor a relic of a bygone industrial era. In 2016, of course, this gamble went up in flames spectacularly. Though Chuck Schumer had boasted, "For every blue-collar Democrat we will lose in western Pennsylvania, we will pick up two or three moderate Republicans in the suburbs of Philadelphia," he had miscalculated the numerical and geographical advantage of the new suburban voting bloc. According to Richard Martin, the Rust Belt manufacturing counties that Schumer had been so eager to cast aside still contained 40 percent of all voters in the US. While Democrats had managed to make inroads in a few Republican-leaning areas that year, the party's losses in midsize manufacturing counties overwhelmed their gains in urban and suburban areas by over 2 million votes.

But even as this strategy yielded disastrous electoral consequences for Democrats, party insiders and political commentators alike continued to cling fast to the dream of a Democratic coalition made up of "highly educated professional whites, especially women, and minority voters," in the words of strategist Lee Drutman.[58] The future Democratic base, Drutman insisted, would consist of "essentially the Obama coalition, but with more of an emphasis on diversity and tolerance, and even more of a role for wealthy cosmopolitans." Working-class whites, on the other hand, could be safely cast aside for the Republicans' taking. In fact, any efforts by Democrats to appeal to working-class voters at all, commentator Monica Potts argued in 2022, were really only overtures to these obsolete whites and therefore likely to flop.[59] "The dividing line in the American electorate is not economics; it's race and culture," she wrote.

Indeed, over the last decade, it's been college-educated whites—a voting bloc that leaned Republican even through Obama's second presidential run—who have steadily flocked to the Democratic Party, bringing with them all the cultural influence (and campaign contributions) that their affluence entails.[60] Astonishingly, by the 2022 midterm elections, Democrats drew greater support from this group than from non-white voters of *any* educational background.[61] But the flipside of the massive advantage Democrats now enjoy with college-educated white voters has been a worrying drift of voters of color *away* from the party. To be clear, majorities of Hispanic, Asian, and particularly black voters have continued to back Democrats in most national and state-level elections. Yet exit polls have also shown that between 2016 and 2020, Trump increased his vote share with each of these groups, despite the fiery summer of racial reckoning and four years of liberal pundits emphasizing the president's racism at every turn. "Democrats have lost ground among nonwhite voters in almost every election over the last decade, even as racially charged fights over everything from a border wall to kneeling during the national anthem might have been expected to produce the exact opposite result," *New York Times* reporter Nate Cohn noted in 2023.[62]

More troubling still for the party was that non-white voters without college degrees were defecting at an even greater clip than their college-educated counterparts. According to the Pew Research Center, 41 percent of Hispanic voters without college degrees voted for Trump in 2020, compared to only 30 percent of college-educated Hispanic voters.[63] A *New York Times* analysis also revealed that Trump dramatically increased his vote share among a number of working-class immigrant enclaves that year, ranging from Vietnamese neighborhoods in Orange County to majority-Hispanic precincts in Chicago to Texas border towns.[64] Drawing from several surveys, long-time Democratic pollster Ruy Teixeira furthermore estimated that support for Democrats among voters of color without college degrees—the non-white working class, you might call them—declined by a staggering 33 points between 2012 and 2022.[65] Just as one key bloc of the promised Democratic base materialized, the loyalty of several other necessary constituencies had begun to fracture.

By the 2024 election, the fissures in the party's base had widened enough to deliver Trump not only the electoral college, for a second time, but also the popular vote. In a year of high inflation and continued public pessimism over the state of the economy, Kamala Harris—whose campaign flashily garnered support from celebrities and billionaires but for working people offered little more than tepid promises of an "opportunity economy"—lost every swing state. Exit polls that year revealed that only 65 percent of the non-white working class had cast ballots for Harris—still a majority, but a drastic decrease from the 73 percent that had backed Biden four years earlier.[66] Democratic support among Hispanic voters in particular cratered, falling some fourteen points from 2020; Trump outright won twelve of fourteen working-class majority-Hispanic counties along the South Texas border, an area that had been considered a Democratic stronghold since the 1970s.[67] Most damningly, Democrats lost households earning under $50,000 a year, as well as households earning between $50,000 and $100,000, while simultaneously winning households making over $100,000 annually. "It should come as no great surprise that a Democratic Party which has abandoned working-class people would find that the working class has abandoned them," Bernie Sanders wrote in an acidic statement the day after the election.

This political realignment not only portends more electoral defeats for the Democrats in the near future but also threatens to constrict the party's longer-running economic priorities. As historian Matthew Karp observed before the election, "A party that wins 60 percent support from the wealthiest 10 percent of the country and 75 percent support from top earners in business and finance and that claims enthusiastic allegiance from much of the billionaire class will not organize a new New Deal."[68] And as party leaders continue to rally around the preferences and sensibilities of their capitalist and professional-managerial class backers, Democrats will find themselves on the back foot in the perpetual corrosive culture wars waged by a Republican Party undergoing its own internal disarray in the atrophying neoliberal order.

4
THE CULTURE WAR VOID

Just before the 2022 midterms, a fledgling political group began circulating ads warning of an insidious new kind of preferential treatment practiced by a Democratic Party preoccupied with racial equity. "Joe Biden and left-wing officials are engaged in widespread racial discrimination against WHITE and ASIAN Americans . . . even though it's against the law," read one of its mailers.

The dispatch had come from the America First Legal Foundation, an organization that envisioned itself as the right's "long-awaited answer to the ACLU."[1] Founded the prior year by Stephen Miller—the Trump advisor and far-right ideologue who had engineered the administration's hardline immigration policies—the group was determined to bring culture war to the courts and hamstring the Biden presidency wherever possible; their activities ranged from filing injunctions to prevent transgender students from playing on high school girls' teams to suing various state departments for the release of classified information on Hunter Biden, the scandal-ridden son of the president and perennial target of the right.

America First Legal's signature lawsuits, however, concerned racial discrimination, or, as they liked to put it, "anti-white bigotry."[2] In its first year alone, the group successfully tanked a pair of controversial race-targeted Covid relief measures, one a debt-relief program for non-white farmers and the other a fund for struggling restaurants that gave explicit preference to minority-owned businesses. America First Legal argued that in both cases whites had been unconstitutionally denied aid on the basis of their race, and in the legal quagmires that followed, the federal programs were shuttered. By the next year, the group—now widely considered part of an "administration-in-waiting" for a Trump 2024 victory—had raised over $44 million and filed a battery of complaints with the federal Equal Employment Opportunity Commission against companies like Kellogg's, NASCAR, and Starbucks (among many others), alleging that their DEI programs were discriminatory against whites (and, on occasion, Jews and Asians as well).[3]

This legal offensive was just one prong of a bitter culture war over race in America that broke out after the turbulent summer of 2020. As Democrats and Democratic-aligned cultural institutions rallied around the mission of racial reckoning, the right swiftly responded with an assault on "wokeness," their media-baiting blanket term for the style of didactic social justice activism that had come to be associated with progressive causes, particularly 2020's protests. According to Republicans, wokeness was overrunning college campuses, corrupting corporate America, and even undermining the strength and global reputation of the US abroad. A handful of Republican politicians, such as Florida governor Ron DeSantis, soon made the defeat of this scourge central to their agendas. "We fight the woke in the legislature. We fight the woke in the schools. We fight the woke in the corporations. We will never, ever surrender to the woke mob," DeSantis proclaimed after winning reelection in 2022. "Florida is where woke goes to die."[4]

To progressives, this war on wokeness (not to mention the disparaging use of the term "woke" itself) was an extension of the same type of white grievance politics that had propelled Trump to the presidency in 2016. In the aftermath of the racial justice protests of 2020, commentators argued, the right-wing attacks on DEI programs and "critical race theory" in schools were simply efforts to shore up white supremacy and reinstate the very social order that the racial reckoning had challenged. "This is a post–George Floyd backlash," Kimberlé Crenshaw told the *New Yorker*.[5]

But if the culture war waged by the right was indeed a pointed political reaction to the wave of racial equity statements and DEI initiatives that had proliferated over 2020, it was also a symptom of the profound decay of the neoliberal order and the declining influence of its most loyal stewards on both sides of the aisle. The pitched partisan conflict over race that escalated in the wake of the Floyd protests was less a reflection of a white racial backlash or an inherently polarized America teetering on the brink of a second Civil War than it was a dismal indication of the two major parties' inability or unwillingness to deliver much of anything for most Americans in the twenty-first century.

Under Pressure

Despite the chokehold that the Democrats and Republicans maintain on American politics, the two parties are themselves paradoxically both institutionally weak. Unlike political parties in much of the rest of the world, America's two parties notably lack formal members who pay dues, elect party leadership, and directly vote on party policy agendas. In this absence of an official card-carrying membership, the parties operate less as proper institutions and more as decentralized networks of donors, voters, and politicians loosely bound by their political and ideological leanings. "Today's parties are hollow parties, neither organizationally robust beyond their roles raising money nor meaningfully felt as a real, tangible presence in the lives of voters or in the work of engaged activists," political scientists Daniel Schlozman and Sam Rosenfeld have observed.[6]

This disorganization has furthermore rendered both parties highly susceptible to the influence of big money. Particularly in the post–Citizens United era of unencumbered political spending, it's the obscenely rich—rather than average voters—who exert outsized influence on the direction and priorities of the parties. The combination of the US open primary system and its lax campaign finance laws has enabled wealthy donors and their PACs to sway election outcomes simply by directing huge sums of money to their preferred candidates. As scholar Paul Heideman has noted, in the case of the Republican Party, this process has generated a perpetual tug-of-war between the party's establishment leaders and far-right insurgents that has pushed the Republicans further and further to the right over time.[7] Over the last several decades, Heideman writes, GOP leadership has been essentially powerless to stop "extreme candidates who run for nomination on its ballot line, particularly if they are well financed."

Today's Republican Party is awash in dark money and has little compunction enacting its preferred policies through the brute force of minoritarian rule. Practices designed to split or suppress Democratic votes—from gerrymandering and restrictive voter identification laws to flat-out election denialism—are a standard part of the Republican electoral strategy. The party moreover thrives on government dysfunction, a position that ensures GOP legislators the upper hand in nearly every congressional standoff, and particularly during government shutdowns, which immobilize sections of the federal government (and, by extension, many public employees' salaries).

But despite this ruthless approach to elections and governance, the Republican Party's longstanding institutional weaknesses have been compounded over the last several decades by ideological shifts within the GOP's voter base that party leaders have struggled to contain. The once-formidable Reagan coalition—which the former president himself famously characterized as a "three-legged stool" made up of free marketeers, social conservatives, and defense hawks—began to splinter following George W. Bush's disastrous and lengthy wars in Afghanistan and Iraq and the increasingly obvious failure of trickle-down economics to deliver prosperity to working people. In 2016, Trump upended a handful of Republican pieties and antagonized party leaders not only by openly condemning the Iraq War and past free trade agreements, but also by pledging to protect Medicare and Social Security, a position anathema to a party long ruled by austerity-minded fiscal conservatives. Since then, several core beliefs of the Reagan-era Republican Party have continued to crumble among the base: According to a *New York Times* poll, by 2023, less than a third of Republican voters said they preferred reducing the national deficit to protecting entitlements (compared to a majority of 62 percent in 2005), and even fewer supported military interventions abroad.[8]

In other words, just as the changing class composition of the Democrats' base has presented them with a number of electoral obstacles, Republicans have been subject to their own mounting disorganization. The tension between a voter base no longer convinced of the core tenets of Reaganism and the party's continued dependence on big donors and business interests still wedded to neoliberalism has left the GOP largely unable to construct a coherent agenda around which to unite the party. That dilemma has spurred Republican politicians to direct more time and energy to cultivating various culture war battles, which unfailingly draw media attention and present opportunities for the right to assail the Democratic Party as elitist and condescending, particularly on social issues.

The Specter Haunting the GOP

The conservative backlash to 2020's racial reckoning found one of its first mainstream conduits in Tucker Carlson's Fox show the September after the summer's protests. That month, guest Christopher Rufo, then a little-known conservative activist, joined Carlson to discuss a sinister left-wing ideology spreading through America. "Critical race theory," Rufo warned, "has become, in essence, the default ideology of the federal bureaucracy and is now being weaponized against the American people." According to Rufo, CRT—"an academic discipline that holds that the United States is a nation founded on white supremacy and oppression, and that these forces are still at the root of our society," as he later put it—had infiltrated government agencies, corporate board rooms, and public school curricula alike.[9]

The interview caught the attention of then president Trump, who was so taken by Rufo's call to arms that he invited him to a meeting at the White House and soon thereafter announced the creation of the 1776 Project, a federal measure intended to preserve "patriotic education" in public schools—and a clear riposte to the *New York Times*' celebrated 1619 Project. The media-savvy Rufo quickly ascended to right-wing stardom and handed Republicans a cause célèbre tailor-made for the era of racial reckoning. Prominent GOP politicians soon incorporated the fight against critical race theory into their campaigns: In 2022, during his bid for governor of Virginia, Republican Glenn Youngkin declared at a campaign stop, "It all starts with curriculum. The curriculum has gone haywire."[10] Immediately upon winning election, he signed an executive order to eliminate CRT from the state's public schools.

From the very beginning of this right-wing crusade, journalists and educators had pointed out that critical race theory proper—a branch of graduate-level legal studies—was not, in fact, being taught in public primary schools. This technicality turned out not to matter much at all; according to Rufo, the fuzziness of the term was its strength. "The goal is to have the public read something crazy in the newspaper and immediately think 'critical race theory,'" he wrote on Twitter.[11] "We have decodified the term and will recodify it to annex the entire range of cultural constructions that are unpopular with Americans." He was similarly forthcoming about his ambitions to put this new boogeyman to work in the service of the age-old Republican goal of destroying public education and shrinking the size of government. "To get universal school choice, you really need to operate from a premise of universal public school distrust," he said in a speech at an Idaho college.[12] He also told the *New Yorker* that he wanted to leverage the controversy over CRT to "politicize the bureaucracy" for the purpose of eventually replacing "essentially corrupted state agencies" with right-wing versions.[13]

But if appending cultural anxieties to a broader attack on public education was standard fare for the party, Republican culture warriors also soon found themselves fighting somewhat more unexpected battles. Incensed by the wave of corporate DEI programs and racial justice statements that had proliferated over the summer of 2020, the party of big business developed a curious interest in curtailing corporate power, or, as they dubbed it, "woke capitalism." In Florida, Ron DeSantis railed against corporations taking stances on racial justice and LGBTQ rights and moved to strip Disney of its special self-governing status after the company publicly opposed a controversial law that restricted discussions of sexuality in schools.[14] Republican politicians in other states advanced similar legislation to punish corporations and investors who signaled support for diversity, abortion, or gun control. According to Reuters, in 2022 alone, Republicans introduced forty-four such laws across seventeen states; Texas, for instance, passed a law barring any business "boycotting" energy companies or "discriminating" against the firearms industry from doing new business with the state, a rule that ultimately barred a number of large investors like Chase, Goldman Sachs, and Bank of America from the state's municipal bond market.[15]

Republicans, in other words, were suddenly in the awkward position of having to condemn corporate America's incursion into politics after spending the better part of a century eagerly bulldozing a path for business to act with impunity. Some stubborn adherents of market freedom tried to resolve this dissonance by insisting that the latest expressions of woke capitalism were, in fact, not capitalism at all. Corporate activism, economists at one libertarian think tank ominously warned, was a movement designed to "diminish economic freedom, the key to prosperity, and push us closer towards a new brand of socialism."[16]

A collection of right-wing literature emerged to confirm that corporate wokeness was just Marxism by another name. Books such as Mark Levin's *American Marxism*, James Lindsay's *Race Marxism: The Truth About Critical Race Theory and Practice*, and Rufo's own contribution, *America's Cultural Revolution: How the Radical Left Conquered Everything*, argued that modern-day wokeness had originated with the Frankfurt School, a group of left-wing intellectuals that had immigrated to the US from Germany during and after World War II and included philosophers Herbert Marcuse and Theodor Adorno. The Frankfurt

School, conservative critics argued, viewed Western capitalist society as inherently oppressive and repressive, a perspective that would inspire later scholars such as Angela Davis—a former student of Marcuse's—and proponents of critical race theory like Derrick Bell and Kimberlé Crenshaw to popularize the notion that America was "rooted in" racism and white supremacy. According to this right-wing account, leftists from the postwar period on undertook what German socialist Rudi Dutschke called the "long march through the institutions," a slow but steady radical ideological takeover of America's government, schools, and even businesses. The result of this decades-long strategy was gradual Marxist indoctrination at the highest levels of American society.

Though the goal of this right-wing intellectual history is, of course, polemic rather than accuracy—*American Marxism* author Mark Levin, for instance, has referred to the "Franklin" School on several occasions—there's nevertheless a kernel of truth in the claim that the Frankfurt School begat a form of "cultural Marxism" that continues to influence left-wing activism today.[17] In the 1960s and '70s, the writings of Marcuse and others did, in fact, inform the social movements of the New Left, which, in turn, have shaped most of the antiracist and feminist frameworks popular today. But the Frankfurt School's most striking legacy in this regard is less its success in smuggling Marxism into mainstream American life and more its *departure* from the traditional Marxist understanding of the working class as the subject of history. The Frankfurt School theorists, author Stuart Jeffries notes, had concluded that "an economic account of history was inadequate; what was needed was a cultural analysis of authoritarianism, racism and the role of mass entertainment in seducing the masses into desiring their own domination."[18] This view ultimately helped underwrite the New Left's dismissal of organized labor for the notion of a new political vanguard comprised of the world's most oppressed—anticolonial Third World guerrillas and the black urban poor in the US—along with radicalized youth.

The implausible claim that Marxism has somehow managed to overrun a country with the highest rates of inequality and the weakest labor protections in the industrialized world is an attempt to conjure a twenty-first-century Red Scare and shock new life into a now-obsolete Cold War paradigm in which the ominous specter of Soviet communism united conservatives and helped suppress or preempt domestic left-wing opposition. But invoking the threat of communism for political ends more than a century after the formation of the Soviet Union and three decades after the fall of the Berlin Wall appears to be a strategy with steeply diminishing returns. Though Republicans have sought to tar everything from the Affordable Care Act to Biden's infrastructure bill to corporate DEI as socialism, today it's self-identified democratic socialist Bernie Sanders—not any of the holdover cold warriors in the Republican Party—who consistently polls as one of the most popular and trusted politicians in America, suggesting that Red Scare–style charges have failed to move much of the public.

By the lead-up to the 2024 presidential election, even stalwart Republican voters had seemingly lost interest in the culture wars amid more pressing concerns like grocery and gas prices. The Republican fixation on wokeness at this point had turned slightly frantic as GOP politicians undertook a series of bizarre witch hunts to root out "wokeness" among federal employees, and conservative commentators attempted to blame DEI for everything from the collapse of the Silicon Valley Bank to Putin's invasion of Ukraine to loose bolts on Boeing planes.[19] Ron DeSantis and entrepreneur and *Woke Inc.* author Vivek Ramaswamy—two politicians who had made anti-wokeness central to their political brands—had entered the presidential race in 2023 to much fanfare from conservative media networks. But by the night of the first Republican primary debate, the topic was polling so badly with Republican voters that none of the candidates on stage would mention it at all, save one or two throwaway lines that drew only halfhearted applause.[20] Within a few short months, both candidates would exit the race and dutifully line up behind Trump, who had, just the summer before, brushed off the very word itself. "I don't like the term *woke*," Trump said at an Iowa rally. "It's just a term they use. Half the people can't define it; they don't know what it is."

The Submerged Electorate

The flimsiness of the GOP's culture war salvoes could have presented an opportunity for Democrats to foreground their commitments to more substantive policies, such as rebuilding America's crumbling infrastructure, restoring the child tax credit, and lowering prescription drug prices. Instead, a number of Democratic Party leaders and commentators chose to engage directly on the right's terms.

In 2022, *New York Times* columnist Jamelle Bouie argued that Rufo's and other conservative activists' explicit animus toward public education and federal programs meant that the cultural fight was inseparable from the defense of public goods.[21] "These are not distractions to ignore; they are battles to be won," he wrote. "The culture war is here, whether Democrats like it or not. The only alternative to fighting it is losing it."

Several progressive members of Congress had the same inclination. "Critical race theory is important, particularly as it relates to education, because it will play an essential role in our process of healing, truth, and reconciliation with the ills that plague our country and lead to unnecessary pain and suffering for Black Americans," New York representative Jamaal Bowman wrote on his social media platforms.[22] In a CNN interview, Alexandria Ocasio-Cortez argued that the Republican antipathy toward CRT was nothing more than an attempt to sweep any and all discussions about race under the rug.[23] "We should say, 'Why don't you want our schools to teach antiracism?' Why don't Republicans want their kids to know the tradition of antiracism in the United States?" she said.

There was, however, no Democrat more committed to the culture war than California governor (and rumored presidential aspirant) Gavin Newsom. In the spring of 2022, as the price of gas in California passed $6 per gallon and a statewide housing crisis continued to spiral, Newsom took to social media to display a picture of himself posing introspectively with a copy of Toni Morrison's *Beloved*, which had become a conspicuous symbol in the ongoing battles over school curricula. "Reading some banned books to figure out what these states are so afraid of," he mused.[24] The next year he took the fight to the television circuit, facing off against Ron DeSantis in a showy "Red

State vs. Blue State" debate on Fox News, a much-hyped yet largely empty spectacle that drew fewer than half the viewers of the first Republican primary debate a few months earlier.[25] Apparently unsatisfied with just one event, Newsom then appeared on *Late Night with Seth Meyers* to take additional shots at DeSantis's anti-woke legislative efforts.[26] "What he really means," Newsom proclaimed, "is anti-black."

For politicians on both sides of the aisle, these types of culture war skirmishes are welcome opportunities to raise one's public profile (not to mention solicit donations) while titillating their existing fans and foes alike. Media outlets chasing views, clicks, and subscriptions have similar incentives to spotlight partisan bickering over race or gender and all the controversial soundbites they inevitably produce. But when it comes to engaging the majority of the electorate, fanning the flames of the culture wars or insisting that cultural issues function as proxies for economic issues only exacerbates what political scientists Peter A. Hall, Georgina Evans, and Sung In Kim have called a "representation gap" in the political system.[27]

Since the 1990s, the Democratic and Republican parties have converged to a startling degree on economic policy, thanks to the Democrats' eager embrace of neoliberalism. The party's rightward drift on economics famously reached its apex during the Clinton administration, even as most remember the time as a period of intense political polarization. As historian Gary Gerstle has pointed out, the highly public animosity between Clinton and Republican Speaker of the House Newt Gingrich in the '90s had the effect of concealing their cooperation on key pieces of neoliberal economic policy, including the deregulation of the telecommunications sector and the repeal of Glass-Steagall. "Their behind-the-scenes collaboration made possible the triumph of the neoliberal order," Gerstle notes.[28] The same reverence for the market and its winners persisted through Obama's bank bailout and Biden's 2020 campaign-trail overtures to Wall Street. "No one's standard of living would change. Nothing would fundamentally change," Biden assured a group of wealthy donors at an Upper East Side fundraising event.

Over the same period that Democrats have moved to the right on economics, however, the two parties have also grown more dissimilar on cultural issues such as abortion, guns, immigration, and race, which is to say that the most salient and visible differences between the two parties since the Clinton era have been cultural rather than economic. One troubling consequence of this simultaneous convergence on economics and divergence on culture is that there now exists a substantive and still-growing section of the electorate that lacks a political party that represents both their economic *and* cultural views. Hall, Evans, and Kim have estimated that over 20 percent of the electorate today can be described as fairly liberal on economic issues such as wages, taxes, and the social safety net while moderate or even conservative on the social ones, including abortion, immigration, and race.[29] (This is, of course, exactly the opposite of the standard libertarian-leaning position—"socially liberal but fiscally conservative"—that continues to dominate mainstream policy and media circles, which helps explains why the economically-liberal-yet-socially-conservative perspective usually goes unmentioned and unheard.)

To put it another way, at least a fifth of the American population skews to the left of Republicans and even centrist Democrats on economics, but simultaneously holds more culturally conservative—or at least more culturally ambivalent—views than the typical twenty-first-century progressive. This unrepresented part of the electorate, Hall, Evans, and Kim further note, is disproportionately made up of manual and service-sector workers without college degrees. It stands to reason that the widening representation gap in the American party system is one reason why political participation among these workers has declined so precipitously between the 1990s and present day. "By 2018, about 60 percent of workers in production, crafts and trades, and lower-level services were expressing little or no interest in politics," the authors write.[30]

While college-educated Democrats often imagine the economically-liberal-yet-socially-conservative voter as a blue-collar white worker with regressive views on race and gender— "the Archie Bunker voter," as MSNBC host Joy Ann Reid has often put it—this particular political orientation also happens to describe a significant number of black, Hispanic, and Asian voters in the US. Black voters, for instance, express lower levels of support for same-sex marriage than other racial groups, while Asian voters as a group have been least enthusiastic about legalizing recreational marijuana.[31] And as pollster Ruy Teixeira has noted, Hispanic voters hold more moderate views on immigration and racial justice than Democrats frequently assume—for instance, a majority of Hispanics oppose ideas like defunding the police or reparations for slavery—and instead overwhelmingly say their primary concerns are the economy, jobs, and health care.[32]

Opinion polling, in fact, consistently confirms that the economy, jobs, health care, and programs like Social Security and Medicare are the top stated priorities not only of Hispanics but of working-class voters of *all* races, including the working-class whites that liberals have insisted are primarily motivated by cultural or racial resentments. Mike Lux, a Democratic strategist who surveyed white working-class voters in small and midsized manufacturing towns after 2016, observed that among this group, culture wars turned most potent in the absence of a strong economic program—that is, the conundrum that Democrats had created for themselves by moving right on economics. "There is danger in the culture war, but economics trump culture wars," Lux wrote in a 2022 report.[33] "In terms of the things working-class voters in these counties care the most about, are most focused on, are most passionate about, it is economics, not culture war debates."

And if culture war fights over issues like abortion and race continue to turn out plenty of voters in elections, an even greater number of Americans appear to be put off by the rancorous partisan theater they generate. According to Gallup, the percentage of people who identify as political independents, rather than as Democrats or Republicans, has spiked since the early '90s.[34] Self-identified independents first started to overtake both Democrats and Republicans in 1991, when the number of Americans who identified as independents was about 36 percent, just a little over the 33 percent who identified as Republicans and the 31 percent who identified as Democrats. By 2023, however, a staggering 49 percent of Americans said they identified as independents—about as much as Democrats (25 percent) and Republicans (25 percent) put together.[35]

Party Identification, Annual Averages, 1988–2021

In politics, as of today, do you consider yourself a Republican, a Democrat, or an independent?

— % Democrat   — % Independent   ···· % Republican

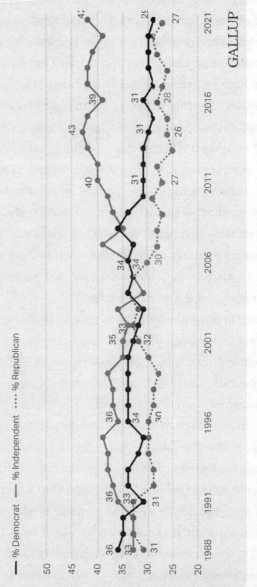

GALLUP

Based on annual averages of Gallup telephone survey interview data. Source: Jeffrey M. Jones, "U.S. Party Preferences Evenly Split in 2022 after Shift to GOP," Gallup News, 12 January 2023, news.gallup.com.

As the graph opposite shows, independent identification and disillusionment with the two major parties began climbing even faster after 2008, the year the country sank into the Great Recession and millions of families lost jobs and homes in the foreclosure crisis. Faced with the staggering human cost of the economic crash, the Obama administration bailed out the banks and left working people hanging even though a majority of voters said they supported government protection from foreclosures. By 2016, economist Matt Stoller observed, "75 percent of voters were looking for someone who could take the country back 'from the rich and powerful,' something unlikely to be done by members of the party that let the financiers behind the 2008 financial crisis walk free."[36] Though some voters took a gamble that year on the confrontational and freewheeling Trump, who had run as a DC outsider on a pledge to drain the swamp, an even greater number sat out the election entirely: That year, close to 100 million citizens declined to vote.[37]

Even more than the rise in independent identification, the chronic abstention of millions from state-level and national elections is perhaps the greatest indictment of the two parties' lackluster offerings. More concerning still, as political scientists Jan Leighley and Jonathan Nagler have observed, is that these nonvoters tend to hold very different views on economics than those who regularly vote.[38] "The one consistent finding from 1972 up through 2008 and in subsequent elections are that voters and nonvoters have different preferences on economic policies," Leighley told NPR in 2018.[39] Multiple studies have shown, for instance, that nonvoters are significantly more supportive than regular voters of measures like minimum wage increases and expanded social safety net benefits.[40] In 2019, one research group in California found that compared to residents who voted regularly, California residents who didn't vote said they preferred a bigger government, more spending on public services, and more government action to reduce inequality.[41]

But according to Leighley and Nagler, one major reason why such people, and particularly those who are lower income, decline to cast ballots is because they don't perceive meaningful differences between Democrats and Republicans. A 2020 Knight Foundation survey of 12,000 nonvoters similarly found that many simply saw the decision not to vote as a rational one.[42] Nonvoters, the study found, were more likely than regular voters to "suffer from a lack of faith in the election system and have serious doubts about the impact of their own votes." They were more likely to believe that the system was rigged.

This cynicism, of course, is far from unfounded. As political scientists Martin Gilens and Benjamin Page detailed in a landmark 2014 study, legislators have been so disproportionately responsive to the policy preferences of economic elites and business lobbyists that the influence of the average citizen on policymaking in the US is essentially zero.[43] "Even big majorities—60 to 80 percent of Americans—get the policy changes they want only about 40 percent of the time," they said in a *Washington Post* interview.[44] "This has real consequences. Millions of Americans are denied government help with jobs, incomes, health care, or retirement pensions. They do not get action against climate change or stricter regulation of the financial sector or a tax system that asks the wealthy to pay a fair share. On all these issues, wealthy Americans tend to want very different things than average Americans do. And the wealthy usually win."

The result of this de facto sidelining of so many people from the political process has been a disheartening feedback loop in which a huge bloc of citizens who are amenable to government interventions to redistribute wealth and reduce inequality are the very same group that's most rapidly losing faith in the political system's ability to deliver such reforms. The culture wars only further shroud this predicament in a dense fog of hyperpartisan conflict that comes off as extreme political polarization but, in fact, conceals a *lack* of choices for voters. While cultural battles reliably stir the most vocal sections of each party's (shrinking) base and supply the media with an endless stream of headlines and opinion pieces, they're a last resort in an era where both parties are struggling to deliver concrete benefits to their constituents amid increasing political disengagement and a floundering neoliberal order.

The Dead End of Right-Wing Populism

In 2023, in an effort to stop Trump from running away with the Republican presidential nomination yet again, some GOP leaders attempted an explicit return to Reaganism. Former vice president Mike Pence briefly entered the primary fray as a "Reagan conservative" and encouraged a party-wide rebuke of his former boss: "We have to resist the siren song of populism unmoored to conservative principles," he said.[45] This, of course, turned out to be a futile and short-lived project.

Only a few months after issuing his challenge, Pence bowed out of the race. That same month, Trump acolytes in Congress staged a contentious ouster of establishment Republican Kevin McCarthy as speaker of the House, securing the former president's continued dominance over the GOP.

With the collapse of the Reagan coalition, some strategists have argued that the path to restoring the Republican Party instead runs through the embrace of non-college-educated voters and the promotion of a working-class agenda that can appeal to them. "Despite the chaos that surrounds Trump and the party's congressional leadership, the Republican coalition is stronger than it was a decade ago—when it was defined by sober-minded figures like John McCain, Paul Ryan and Romney," Republican pollster Patrick Ruffini has insisted.[46] "Working-class populism gives Republicans the opportunity to build a more broadly based party based in the working and middle classes."

This has been the hope of a growing group of conservative politicians and analysts who have eagerly interpreted the drift of voters without college degrees away from the Democrats as a sign of a newly emerging Republican majority made up of the "multiracial working class," as Florida senator Marco Rubio has put it. Inspired by the runaway success of Trump, legislators like Josh Hawley and J. D. Vance and cultural figures like Tucker Carlson have sought to accelerate this realignment by advocating a right-wing populist agenda anchored to a program of economic nationalism and a revival of domestic manufacturing. "We've got to be the party of working people. We've got to be the party of getting jobs back in this country.

We've got to be the party of higher wages for working people," Hawley said in a 2021 Fox News interview.[47] "And we need new opportunities for people to get job-training skills without having to pay for an expensive four-year education that they don't want."

The intellectual ballast of this current proworker wing of the Republican Party is American Compass, a think tank founded by former Mitt Romney adviser Oren Cass. The group announced its arrival on Labor Day of 2020 with a public call for a new program of conservative economic populism. Their inaugural publication—which was titled "Conservatives Should Ensure Workers a Seat at the Table" and endorsed by Rubio, Hawley, and Jeff Sessions, among other GOP leaders—argued that laissez-faire capitalism had failed the average American worker and was due for an overhaul.[48] "Strong worker representation can make America stronger," the brief declared. Since then, American Compass has gone on to champion reforms that break decisively from neoliberal principles, including a monthly child tax credit for working parents, closing the US trade deficit, and major government investment in the revitalization of manufacturing in the US. The organization is a small but increasingly influential force on the right; according to the conservative journalist Christopher Caldwell, "Nearly all the Republicans loosely aligning themselves with working-class interests listen to Cass."[49]

It's one thing, however, to recognize the appeal of a platform of good jobs and high wages, the reshoring of manufacturing, and strengthened collective bargaining rights. It's quite another to form a right-wing party that can actually deliver on those promises. Republicans attempting to craft or advance any kind of meaningful proworker agenda will necessarily come up against the steadfastly antiunion business interests that still exert massive influence on the party. Despite the recent fulminations of some conservatives against "woke capitalism," the Republican Party remains beholden to a ruling class that has no intention of relinquishing any of its power. Billionaire donor Charles Koch, for example, has notoriously funneled billions of dollars into elections for decades to promote a fiercely free market agenda. This money continues to hold such sway over Republican policymaking that journalist Jane Mayer characterized the Koch network in her book *Dark Money* as a "rival center of power to the Republican establishment."

Another inconvenient obstacle to Republican populism appears to be the Republican base itself. Though an increasing number of Republican voters have soured on market fundamentalism, most simultaneously still oppose the kinds of policies that could begin to reverse four decades of inequality. In 2023, American Compass released the results of a poll of registered Republicans that purported to reveal the emergence of a "new conservative voter" that had "abandoned the traditional Republican Party focus on tax cuts, deregulation, and free trade."[50] But even as survey respondents overwhelmingly agreed that the middle class had been squeezed and that wages had stagnated, they remained hostile to unions, tax increases, and social welfare policies. Seventy-four percent of respondents, for example, said they opposed the idea of a monthly cash benefit for working families with children, and 72 percent agreed with the statement "Politicians should focus on cutting taxes, and never consider raising them." Nearly 60 percent—a clear majority—said they considered unions "a negative force that harm workers, employers, and consumers." In other words, Republican economic populists have not only an uphill battle against powerful donors still aggressively attached to libertarian ideals but also the task of winning over a voter base that may see the shortcomings of trickle-down economics but nevertheless continues to shun organized labor or any kind of government redistribution.

This all but ensures that right-populist policy solutions are toothless at best and counterproductive at worst. In 2022, with the backing of American Compass, Marco Rubio and Indiana representative Jim Banks introduced the Teamwork for Employees and Managers (TEAM) Act, a bill seeking to modify existing labor law to allow employers to create and run "employee involvement organizations," or non-union workers' groups. Though framed by its sponsors as a "proworker labor reform" intended to facilitate cooperation between employees and management, the bill would have in fact undercut labor: For one thing, the type of workers' committees proposed by the TEAM Act—largely symbolic groups with no real leverage in the workplace or voting power on company boards—already currently exist in the form of the employee resource groups that employers frequently count as part of DEI. Worse still was that the legal changes proposed in the TEAM Act would have rolled back existing labor protections by creating a legal loophole for the kinds of employer-run company unions meant to defang and deter actual union organizing.

This muddled attempt at threading the needle between

improving the lot of workers while also preserving their employer's dominance over them evinces the limits of the right's proworker sentiments. Groups like American Compass may genuinely want to revive the American working class, but today this is a goal that necessarily requires major government spending and a political confrontation with big business—not simply populist rhetoric and certainly not any further assaults on the US's already tattered labor laws. "If you're giving workers some say over what happens on the shop floor, in the office, or in the service center, you're limiting the discretionary power of the employer," the labor historian Joshua Freeman once put it.[51] "And it's pretty hard to find a conservative that actually wants to do that."

As it happens, neither American Compass nor any of the self-styled Republican populists in Congress have shown much interest in, for example, adequately funding the cash-strapped and chronically understaffed National Labor Relations Board, let alone backing any kind of legislation that might substantively increase workers' capacity to unionize. The Protecting the Right to Organize (PRO) Act—a measure to roll back statewide right-to-work laws and strengthen collective bargaining protections for workers—passed in the House in 2021 with the support of only five Republicans and has since stalled in the Senate, where it conspicuously lacks the support of Rubio, Hawley, or Vance. The populist right's avoidance of any kind of meaningful reform has been so pronounced that even Sohrab Ahmari, one of its star intellectuals, glumly concluded in 2023, "The Republican Party remains, incorrigibly, a vehicle for the wealthy."[52]

What's perhaps more likely—and, in fact, more dire—than a

multiracial working-class Republican majority in the making is
the further alienation of said multiracial working class from the
political process entirely. As authors Benjamin Fong and Dustin
Guastella have argued, while blue-collar workers angered by
the blunders and betrayals of the Democrats may very well cast
ballots for Republicans over an election cycle or two, there's
no guarantee they'll remain loyal to the GOP over the long
run, especially given that the party has shown itself unlikely
to enact any kind of type of legislation that might reverse the
pernicious effects of inequality or lead to real improvements in
the lives of most working people.[53] The more plausible long-
term outcome of the ongoing working-class exodus from the
Democratic Party is widespread demobilization in a country
where voter turnout is already dismally low compared to other
developed countries, particularly among the poor and working class. This political alienation already appears to be well
under way: In a recent Pew study, a scant 4 percent of the
public said they believed the political system was functioning
well.[54] Despite the rhetorical gestures of American Compass
and its kindred lawmakers, when it comes to attracting and
retaining a decisive share of working-class voters—let alone
operating as a genuine organ for working-class politics—the
Democratic and Republican parties have arrived at a gloomy
stalemate that shows no sign of abating.

The Legacy of Civil Rights

Despite their insistence that wokeness had overtaken America's
institutions, the right notched a major culture war victory in

June of 2023 when the conservative-majority Supreme Court ruled against affirmative action in higher education, officially barring universities from considering race in admissions. "The Court finally got away from the deceptions put up by universities to protect their obsession with racial quotas," one writer for the *National Review* declared triumphantly.[55] "The Supreme Court has struck down affirmative action in college admissions," Christopher Rufo tweeted.[56] "It's time to go further: abolish DEI bureaucracies, prohibit race-based hiring, eliminate the 'disparate impact' doctrine, and restore the principle of colorblind equality in all of our institutions."

Some conservative activists soon attempted to do just that using existing civil rights legislation. In the wake of the Supreme Court's ruling, Edward Blum—the same legal activist behind the cases that had sparked the affirmative action hearing—went on to sue two law firms and a venture capital fund on the grounds that their minority-only fellowships violated the Civil Rights Act of 1866. (Rather than go to court, the law firms opened their fellowships to applicants of all races.) Meanwhile, Stephen Miller's America First Legal inundated the EEOC with complaints that various corporate DEI programs—such as a plan by Macy's to "achieve more ethnic diversity by 2025 at senior director level and above, with a goal of 30 percent"— were in breach of Title VII of the Civil Rights Act of 1964.[57] "This DEI bigotry is sinister, wrong, immoral—and must be defeated," Miller said in a statement.[58]

Others on the right had already taken aim at civil rights law itself. In his 2020 book *The Age of Entitlement*, journalist Christopher Caldwell argued that the 1964 Civil Rights

Act—originally conceived to end the legal apartheid of Jim Crow—had inadvertently come to spawn an endless regime of government-approved social engineering on behalf of not just racial minorities but women, gays, immigrants, and other so-called marginalized groups. This new order, according to Caldwell, turned Americans against each other and effectively consigned whites to the "bottom rung of an official hierarchy of races." In early 2024, the hard-right Claremont Institute, where Caldwell holds a post, released a statement calling for an end to DEI and "diversity fanaticism" based on his interpretation of the law.[59] "The sad truth is that the 1964 Civil Rights Act, and especially its administrative and jurisprudential offspring, have warped American law and culture and traded one set of racial preferences for another," the organization wrote.

Libertarian provocateur Richard Hanania likewise contended in his 2023 book *The Origins of Woke* that the 1964 act had unleashed a new type of government tyranny over the private sector. Drawing from Frank Dobbin's analysis of Title VII, Hanania argued that the vagueness of the antidiscrimination mandate in the Civil Rights Act had created an insidious form of federal soft power that ignited the creation of a vast and oppressive DEI bureaucracy. Since the end of the '60s, Hanania wrote, the omnipresent threat of a federal crackdown in the name of civil rights had effectively forced corporations into a "woke arms race" as they anxiously tried to preempt expensive and embarrassing discrimination lawsuits with increasingly absurd DEI requirements. "Our major corporations came of age in a legal environment in which bureaucrats and courts were on the constant lookout for racism and sexism, and they built an entire section of their workforce in order to address such concerns," he wrote.

What this right-wing conception of the federal civil rights apparatus tends to overlook, however, is the central role of the private sector in shaping antidiscrimination practices *and* their enforcement. As discussed in chapter 2, Dobbin's research shows that the strain of human resources management that would eventually become DEI did initially grow out of companies' efforts to keep in compliance with Title VII. Yet, he also makes clear that the massive expansion of this corporate juggernaut over the last several decades has had little to do with fear of government sanction. In fact, the most critical period of growth for diversity management occurred during the presidency of Ronald Reagan, who slashed funding to the EEOC in an attempt to kill affirmative action (and appointed none other than arch-conservative Clarence Thomas to preside over the hollowed-out agency). Corporate America responded not only by preserving—and expanding—its existing diversity programs but also by urging the administration to reconsider its stance.

It isn't, in other words, the heavy hand of the government or an out-of-control federal civil rights regime that has forced DEI on the citizenry, let alone generated an entire modern-day edifice of "wokeness." Hanania and Caldwell both attribute the spread of antidiscrimination norms to government "regulators" and "the courts," but, as Dobbin writes, the relationship between the judiciary and the private sector on the question of affirmative action and DEI has historically run the other

way. "When bureaucrats or the courts took stands on compliance, most ratified what the Fortune 500 were doing," Dobbin
notes.[60] If the ambiguities of Title VII had generated some
early confusion in the private sector, it had also allowed businesses a great deal of leeway to craft and set their own industry
standards around antidiscrimination practices. As Dobbin put
it, "It was corporations that guided the judiciary, not the other
way around."[61]

Against Hanania's portrayal of a beleaguered corporate
America fighting to keep afloat in a deluge of post-1964 litiga-
tion, discrimination suits are also notoriously difficult for plaintiffs to win (and American labor law, in general, is weighted
heavily in favor of employers). Though over the years a handful
of discrimination cases have resulted in high-profile trials and
large settlements for plaintiffs, these are the exception rather
than the rule. One legal research firm found that plaintiffs who
filed discrimination suits won their cases less than 1 percent
of the time, whereas employers won around 14 percent of the
time.[62] The majority of discrimination suits today, the firm
noted, are dismissed or settled, and even those that result
in out-of-court settlements for plaintiffs aren't necessarily
particularly lucrative after the high cost of legal fees. And
though the EEOC has had the power to file their own suits
since 1972, the agency has been chronically stretched thin. A
2019 investigation by reporters Maryam Jameel and Joe Yeradi
found that, adjusted for inflation, the EEOC had a smaller
budget and 42 percent fewer staff than it did in 1980.[63] They
furthermore noted that the agency closed the vast majority of
cases they received without concluding whether discrimination

had occurred. "Workers receive some form of assistance, such as money or a change in work conditions, only 18 percent of the time," they wrote.

The push to link the sprawl of DEI to government over-reach or the civil rights victories of the postwar period has also left conservatives like Caldwell and Hanania with a set of largely unattainable and politically toxic legislative goals, such as the repeal of the 1964 Civil Rights Act and the destruction of the EEOC. ("No matter how strong the philosophical or practical case is for doing away with anti-discrimination laws in the private sector, political reality means that they are here to stay," Hanania lamented in his book.) There is currently no public appetite for overturning the Civil Rights Act, and, in fact, part of the legacy of the civil rights movement is the near-unanimous belief today among Americans in every citizen's right to legal protection from discrimination and in a colorblind ideal of equality in which no one is hindered *or* helped on the basis of their race. An overwhelming 91 percent of respondents in one 2022 national survey, for instance, agreed with the statement "All people deserve an equal opportunity to succeed, no matter their race or ethnicity."[64]

In the context of the contemporary culture wars, however, this widely shared ideal of colorblind equality among the public has meant that the Democratic Party has also been at odds with voters on the issue of race-conscious admissions. According to Gallup, in 2023, nearly 70 percent of Americans agreed that the Supreme Court's decision to strike down affirmative action was "mostly a good thing."[65] A Pew survey from a few years before the ruling had similarly found that 73 percent of the public—including a majority of every racial group—thought colleges and universities should not consider race or ethnicity in admissions.[66] But in the wake of the ruling, prominent Democrats vocally rallied around the opposite position, with Chuck Schumer calling the decision a "giant roadblock in our country's march toward racial justice" and Massachusetts representative Ayanna Pressley describing it as "the latest in the white supremacist assault on equity in education."[67]

This bifurcation between the views of the Democratic leadership and broad public sentiment had already materialized a few years prior in California, when a majority of voters rejected a ballot measure to restore race-based affirmative action in the state despite the urgings of Democratic leaders across the state to vote yes on the measure. ("The 2020 campaign to restore race-conscious affirmative action in California was close to gospel within the Democratic Party," the *New York Times* wrote.[68]) Hopeful that the summer of racial justice protests would galvanize public support for affirmative action, Democrats poured some $31 million into outreach (outspending the opposition by 19 to 1) and collected prominent endorsements from sports teams and celebrities. But on Election Day, voters in one of the bluest and most diverse states in the nation rejected the measure by a 57-to-43 percent vote.

Progressives often point to the fact that the US has yet to reach a perfect state of colorblindness in order to dismiss the ideal of colorblindness itself. But the widespread belief in the value of colorblind equality or race neutrality among Americans isn't necessarily a denial that discrimination persists or a sign of latent white supremacy so much as it is an indication of the liberalization of racial attitudes made possible by the real (if sometimes slow or halting) integration of workplaces, schools, and neighborhoods since the 1960s. In recent years, conservative activists like Blum and Rufo have sought to take advantage of the broad public consensus on civil rights by rejecting the libertarian fever dream of repealing the 1964 Civil Rights Act and instead advocating a kind of black-letter enforcement of Title VII while challenging newer pieces of civil rights legislation. "The ideological capture of the Civil Rights Act is neither fixed nor inevitable," Rufo wrote in early 2024.[69] "Rather than argue for its abolition, Americans concerned about the excesses of the DEI bureaucracy should appeal to higher principles and demand that our civil rights law conform to the standard of colorblind equality."

But for a Democratic Party still bleeding working-class voters, what's likely more damaging than being outmaneuvered on affirmative action by sensible-seeming Republican opponents is that the very issue of race-conscious college admissions—no matter one's stance—is, by definition, an intra-elite conflict in a country where 60 percent of the population lacks a college degree and the cost of post-secondary education for those who do attend college has grown so astronomical that it's famously generated close to $2 trillion of student debt and jeopardized the financial solvency of even middle-class households.

The fight over diversifying higher education, and especially its most prestigious or selective institutions, in other words, may be an urgent moral matter within college-educated Democratic policy circles seeking to convey their support for racial justice. But at a time of pronounced inequality and widespread public pessimism over the economy, it's a position that has predictably failed to rally Americans contending with immediate concerns like raised costs of living and inflation outpacing wage growth. As one working-class California resident put it when asked by the *New York Times* about the state's affirmative action ballot measure in 2020, "It was a distraction from the issues that affect our lives."[70]

5
THE RETREAT FROM THE UNIVERSAL

In 2016, at the end of his term, then president Barack Obama signed into law a bipartisan bill aimed at stanching the growing opioid epidemic, which had killed an estimated 33,000 people in the US the previous year. The bill, touted as the first major piece of national legislation to address drug addiction in over forty years, authorized $181 million in funding for addiction treatment and prevention. It was, in the words of Republican Ohio senator and bill cosponsor Rob Portman, "the first time that we've treated addiction like the disease that it is, which will help put an end to the stigma that has surrounded addiction for too long."[1]

For some scholars and activists, the congressional attention to the opioid crisis as a public health concern marked a departure from the US's draconian War on Drugs policies and was therefore itself a manifestation of entrenched racial inequality in America.[2] On *PBS NewsHour*, law professor Ekow Yankah contrasted what he viewed as the newly sympathetic rhetoric on opioid deaths to the punitive approach to crack use in the 1990s: "Back then, when addiction was a black problem, there was no wave of national compassion," he said.[3] "White heroin addicts get overdose treatment, rehabilitation, and reincorporation. Black drug users got jail cells and 'just say no.'"

The existence of this racist double standard quickly became a kind of conventional wisdom among progressives. On a 2019 podcast episode titled "A Tale of Two Crises: Opiates vs. Crack," physician and left-wing Michigan politician Abdul El-Sayed argued that the public and legislative response to the opioid epidemic not only illuminated the country's callous indifference to the crack crisis but revealed *the* foundational fault line in American society. "We hear the words 'structural racism,' quite a bit these days," he said. "It's the kind of racism that goes beyond people using racial epithets or denying people of color service. It's the way that race shapes the very contours of American society. The strikingly different responses to crack and opioids is an example of structural racism at play."

It indeed would have been a striking turn for politicians to roll back the decades-long tough-on-crime approach to drugs and replace prison sentences with compassionate addiction treatment once the public face of drug use had shifted from black to white. The problem, however, was that no such turn had occurred at all.

Between 2000 and 2020, the War on Drugs steadily migrated to rural and suburban America, altering the demographics of incarceration. A 2016 *New York Times* investigation found that Dearborn County, Indiana—whose population was approximately 50,000 and more than 97 percent white—sent more people to prison per capita than any other county in the nation. "The extraordinarily high incarceration rate here—about one in 10 adults is in prison, jail or probation—is driven less by crime and poverty than by a powerful prosecutor, hard-line judges and a growing heroin epidemic," the *Times* noted.[4] Over the last decade, in fact, so many white people have gone to prison for drug offenses that it's helped narrow the much-discussed racial disparities in the prison population. "Although the rhetoric has been less harsh at times, the country continues to deploy many of the same punitive weapons and has added some new ones," political scientist Marie Gottschalk observed in 2022.[5] Today, for instance, in response to the deadly spread of fentanyl, several states have increased penalties for possession and distribution of opioids even as they've loosened sentences for marijuana and other drug offenses.

The contention that the opioid epidemic has been met with compassion and care because its primary victims have been white is also a particularly strange one when you consider that at the end of 2020, the US marked a nauseating milestone of more than 90,000 total drug overdose deaths in just one year. (For comparison, overdose deaths during the height of the crack crisis in the '90s numbered around 8,000 per year.) Since 2021, more than 100,000 people have continued to die from overdoses every year. Despite this staggering death toll, addiction treatment options in the United States' byzantine for-profit health care system remain difficult to access and prohibitively expensive, even for those with insurance. As Gottschalk notes, federal legislation intended to combat the opioid crisis—including the much-publicized 2016 bipartisan bill—has barely scratched the surface of the vast epidemic that has already claimed the lives of hundreds of thousands of people and to date shows only minimal signs of slowing. "As opioids have cut a widening swath of destruction across the United States, the government and public policy response has been at best inadequate and misguided, and, at worst, cruel and lethal," she writes.

The conclusion by racial justice advocates that the opioid crisis somehow demonstrates the inherent elevation of white lives over black ones offers just one recent and striking example of how the framework of antiracism, well-intentioned as it may be, so often conceals or mystifies the actual mechanisms that produce inequality and cheapen human life. The function of antiracism—and the explicitly stated goal of self-described antiracists—is to "center" race, that is, to make race and racism the exclusive or principal frame through which American history and politics are understood. But while racial double standards and disparities do continue to exist, the insistence that they represent the very foundation on which American society operates is an obfuscation that grows more and more politically poisonous by the day. Despite its proponents' best intentions, antiracism has led to a host of untenable or short-sighted political solutions—or, at worst, a kind of nihilistic political paralysis—far more often than it has generated constructive politics.

To put it another way, the insistence on centering race in political analysis and policymaking has not brought us any closer to understanding our present conditions, let alone facilitating the kind of majoritarian political coalition that will be necessary to overturn a deeply unequal economy that works for the few at the expense of the many. Contemporary antiracism, even in its supposedly radical forms, continually displaces a universalist approach to social change and, especially after 2020's reckoning, all too often trades mass politics for vanguardism.

Bad History, Bad Solutions

Today racial disparities in society are widely understood as a smoking gun for the existence of an all-encompassing "structural" or "systemic" racism. This interpretation has not only blinded many progressives to the reality of contemporary crises but has, on occasion, managed to rewrite history in ways that further lead away from the kind of large-scale economic reforms that would transfer power to working people and, incidentally, drastically reduce or eliminate many of the racial disparities that have drawn scrutiny in recent times.

In recent years, one frequent target of this type of antiracist historical revisionism has been the New Deal. Though the New Deal constituted the single most comprehensive set of federal policies for the working class in US history, influential twenty-first century works such as Ta-Nehisi Coates's "The Case for Reparations" and Richard Rothstein's *The Color of Law* have helped popularize a conception of the New Deal as a racially exclusionary agenda explicitly designed to benefit white Americans alone—"affirmative action for whites," as historian Ira Katznelson has memorably characterized it. Today Democratic lawmakers have continued to promote this idea, from South Carolina representative Jim Clyburn, who remarked in 2021, "FDR's legacy was not good for Black people. The New Deal was not fair to Black people," to Alexandria Ocasio-Cortez, who described the New Deal in a 2019 interview as "an extremely economically racist policy that drew literal red lines around black and brown communities" and claimed, "Basically, it invested in white America."[6]

The New Deal was, of course, a product of 1930s America, which is to say, by no means perfect or free from racial discrimination. "There is no question that African Americans did not receive their fair share of New Deal programs—particularly in housing," Touré Reed has noted.[7] "But the now commonplace tendency to dismiss the Roosevelt administration's crucial role in improving the material lives of millions of African Americans has obscured both the importance of the New Deal's redistributive policies to blacks—who demonstrated their support for the administration with their votes—and the influence of New Deal liberalism over the scope of black political activism from the 1930s through the civil rights movement." Against the knee-jerk claim that the legislation explicitly codified or exacerbated racial apartheid, black workers participated in (and were, in fact, technically *overrepresented* in many of) the New Deal's public works programs, including the Civilian Conservation Corps, the Works Progress Administration, and the Public Works Administration. The reelection of Roosevelt in 1936 also marked the moment that a critical mass of black voters—formerly reliable supporters of the party of Lincoln—flipped to the Democratic Party. Key pieces of New Deal legislation, such as the Wagner Act, further laid the groundwork for the union organizing that would eventually serve as a critical pipeline to the civil rights movement a few decades later.

But the pop-progressive understanding of the New Deal as deliberately racially exclusionary is now so widespread that it's spawned a set of second-order distortions. In recent years, journalists and commentators have often casually repeated the falsehood that workers ineligible for New Deal programs like Social Security were *predominantly* black: "Cutting out agricultural and domestic workers, a majority of whom were Black, made it easier to win the support of Southern Democrats for Social Security legislation," reads a representative 2022 *New York Times* opinion piece.[8] In fact, while black workers were disproportionately represented among agricultural and domestic workers, the *majority* of these workers—nearly 75 percent, according to Census records—were white. This is a puzzling amount of collateral damage for a program supposedly meant to function as "affirmative action for whites." The numbers, however, start to make some sense when you instead consider the decidedly less titillating account of the genesis of Social Security offered by historian Larry DeWitt, who has argued that most of the political pressure for carving out farm workers and domestic workers from the program came not from Southern Democrats motivated by racial animus, but from business lobbies like the American Farm Bureau, which insisted that paying taxes into the new system would be too burdensome for employers.[9]

Likewise, in a sober discussion on systemic racism with Stephen Colbert at the height of 2020's protests, Jon Stewart proclaimed that the New Deal's GI Bill had been "the most progressive piece of legislation that may have ever happened on the soil of America, and yet it explicitly excluded black people."[10] He was referring to the section of the bill that offered federally insured low-interest home loans to veterans, a benefit that most black GIs were legally entitled to but were ultimately unable to use due to racial discrimination from real estate brokers and mortgage lenders who prevented them from buying homes in the first place. However, even as they were de facto denied the GI Bill's housing benefits, black veterans made use of its educational benefits at a higher rate than their white counterparts (and subsequently expressed higher levels of satisfaction with the program).[11] Positive experiences with this government program during the racially segregated and otherwise unequal Jim Crow era encouraged future civic participation among recipients; like black unionists who had cut their teeth in the labor movement after the Wagner Act, black GI Bill recipients went on to disproportionately populate the civil rights movement. "To ignore this experience is to discount the role of the expanded welfare state in improving the lives of black Americans in the context of extreme racial inequality," labor organizer Paul Prescod has written.[12]

The warped conception that the New Deal was racist or that it worsened racial inequality in the US is not only inaccurate but has also come to run cover for a set of pernicious reiterations of market fundamentalism. As Reed has noted, what ultimately limited the reach and transformative potential of the New Deal was its architects' commitment to appeasing business and preserving capitalism, not their commitment to preserving an abstract white supremacy. Yet the criticism of the New Deal—and its misidentification of the federal government as the driving motor of racial inequality in the postwar period—has functioned to discredit the ideal of broad-based social-democratic reforms while also stoking a particular kind of antigovernment sentiment that unsurprisingly finds fans on the right. In 2023, for instance, two conservative *Wall Street Journal* writers combined a defense of the free market with an attack on the New Deal on the grounds that the latter had interfered with the former at the expense of black Americans. "These and other government policies caused immense economic harm to African-Americans," they wrote, briefly sounding like Alexandria Ocasio-Cortez.[13] "But they aren't capitalism," they concluded. "They're interventions into markets, state-sanctioned theft, and political payoffs to segregationists."

The unwavering focus on redlining as the primary source of the black-white wealth gap—and the identification of the black-white wealth gap as proof of structural racism—has also supplied justifications for destructive, right-wing practices like banking deregulation. In 2023, prominent racial justice advocates joined forces with big banks to challenge an FDIC decision to raise capital requirements on large banks. According to the *Washington Post*, groups such as the NAACP, the National Urban League, and the Urban Institute all opposed the rule on the grounds that it would make loans harder to obtain for black home buyers.[14] In a statement to the FDIC, the executive director of the Milwaukee-based grassroots group Black Leaders Organizing for Communities invoked historical discrimination to argue against greater bank oversight: "Moving forward with these rules would harm communities that have historically struggled to obtain consistent access to banking services and credit lines," she said.[15] "This is especially true for African-American populations in Milwaukee, who have faced decades of redlining, discriminatory lending practices, and other forms of economic disparities."

As *American Prospect* editor David Dayen observed at the time, this was a somewhat curious argument given that the rule would have affected financial giants such as Chase, Goldman Sachs, and Wells Fargo but *not* the non-bank mortgage lenders that currently make up the top mortgage lenders in the US (and are disproportionately used by the type of lower-income home buyers on whose behalf the aforementioned advocacy groups were theoretically speaking).[16] More fundamentally, the emphasis on wealth-building through home ownership—and, specifically, the insistence that greater regulation of financial institutions would disadvantage black would-be homeowners—was reminiscent of the type of free market delirium that had paved the way to the subprime mortgage crisis of 2008.

In the 1990s, in an explicit effort to combat the effects of historical redlining and "the barriers of discrimination," the Clinton administration's Department of Housing and Urban Development launched a major initiative to expand home-ownership among black Americans.[17] The HUD program, which entailed loosening lending standards and lifting a number of regulations on the private mortgage industry, was by many measures a success: By the year 2000, black and Hispanic home-ownership rates had risen twice as fast as they had for whites, and the nation had achieved a record level of homeowner-ship. Clinton's successor George W. Bush eagerly continued the project in the new millennium by relaxing additional regulations as part of a plan to boost credit access and create 5.5 million new minority homeowners.[18] "Today, while nearly three-quarters of all white Americans own their homes, less than half of all African Americans and Hispanic Americans are homeowners," Bush said in a radio address in 2002.[19] "We must begin to close this homeownership gap by dismantling the barriers that prevent minorities from owning a piece of the American dream."

But the very real increase in the number of minority homeowners that resulted from the bipartisan strategy of aggressive deregulation would, of course, prove to be a Pyrrhic victory when the same policies later triggered a catastrophic recession in which millions of families—disproportionately "Black and brown," in contemporary parlance—lost their homes. While Ibram X. Kendi has neatly defined a racist policy as "any measure that produces or sustains racial inequity between racial groups"—and, on the flipside, an antiracist policy as one that "produces or sustains racial equity between racial groups"—the fact that the market-based housing schemes of the '90s and early 2000s resulted in *both* outcomes demonstrates the shortcomings of public policies that seek to ameliorate racial disparities without first altering or constraining the economic forces that produce inequality across the board.

In the case of housing, political scientist Preston H. Smith II has argued that the more important distinction is not whether a policy can be shown to produce racial equity—that is, equal percentages of black and white homeowners—but whether it consolidates or challenges the prevailing market logic in which housing is understood as a commodity. The social-democratic approach that instead treats housing as a right or public good, Smith writes, has all but vanished in the contemporary discourse on redlining, but was actively pursued during the New Deal era by black civic leaders who insisted that antidiscrimination efforts had to be coupled with robust federal interventions to rein in the private real estate industry and expand public housing.[20] As Robert Weaver, an appointee to Roosevelt's so-called Black Cabinet and later Lyndon B. Johnson's HUD secretary, wrote in 1948, "The housing problem of minorities can never be solved or materially lessened until the nation has an effective program for meeting adequately the shelter requirements of all the people." Nearly eighty years later—with more than half of all renters in the US contributing over 30 percent of their income to rent, and homeownership out of reach for millions thanks to soaring housing prices and high mortgage rates—we're clearly still waiting on that program.

Race Targeting in an Economy of Scarcity

On all official measures, the US economy made a dramatic rebound as Covid subsided. By early 2022, GDP was on the rise, the unemployment rate had fallen, and millions of new jobs had opened. Wages were rising across several sectors thanks to the tight labor market, and businesses were enjoying some of the highest profits and profit margins they had seen since the 1950s.

But the public, to the chagrin of the experts, was largely unappreciative of the new era of growth. Opinion polling that year revealed that three-quarters of Americans were pessimistic about the economy despite the encouraging statistics.[21] "There's a huge disconnect between economic reality, which is mixed—inflation is a big concern, but job growth has been terrific—and public perceptions, which are weirdly dismal," Paul Krugman mused in his *New York Times* column.[22] Historian Heather Cox Richardson chalked up the public pessimism to right-wing disinformation: "We are in the greatest economic recovery since WWII," she tweeted.[23] "Maybe the issue is not Biden but right-wing disinformation and those who amplify it."

The gloom, however, was the product of more than just anti-Biden Republican propaganda. Inflation that year had quickly outstripped wage gains, and costs of living across the country continued to rise. "Groceries are up 25% since January 2020. Same with electricity. Used-car prices have climbed 35%, auto insurance 33% and rents roughly 20%," *Bloomberg* reported at the end of 2023.[24] "Housing affordability is at its worst on record, auto-loan rates have soared, and borrowing with a credit card has never been so expensive."

Worse still was that the government appeared mostly indifferent to the soaring costs of living. Though the Biden administration had overseen a much-needed expansion of the social safety net during the pandemic, within a few years it went on to let nearly every one of the new measures lapse though they had been both effective and popular. The expanded child tax credit—a monthly cash benefit for households with children that had lowered the child poverty rate by some 40 percent during the pandemic—expired at the end of 2021, sending an estimated 3.7 million children back into poverty. According to the Census Bureau, by the spring of the next year, more than a third of families with children in the US were struggling to pay bills and cover other basic household costs.[25] The year after that, a Covid measure that had waived eligibility renewals for people enrolled in Medicaid expired, purging nearly 18 million low-income recipients from the rolls.

Even beyond pandemic financial straits, it's little surprise that Americans have been less and less inclined to cheer the official numbers on economic growth given that the middle class has been relentlessly squeezed for the last four decades regardless of GDP fluctuations or which party occupies the White House. The problem with today's economy is not only that an estimated 37 million people still live in poverty in the wealthiest country in the world but also that the government has done painfully little to address longstanding concerns like the skyrocketing costs of childcare, health care, and education. The US still has the distinction of being one of the few rich countries in the world that doesn't guarantee its citizens paid sick leave, paid parental leave, or health care, and the consequence of this state abdication is that even households with two incomes often live just a paycheck or two away from financial disaster. A year or two of on-paper recovery doesn't reverse forty years of widening economic inequality or the replacement of stable middle-income jobs with an explosion of low-wage work.

One logical solution to this continued downward pressure on working people is the revitalization and expansion of the ambitious economic program that began with the New Deal. In the neoliberal era, a number of political efforts—including but certainly not limited to the 1996 Labor Party, which for a time organized several national unions and hundreds of locals around a social-democratic platform, and the 2016 and 2020 Bernie Sanders campaigns, which drew a sizable bloc of voters around the same—have sought to build a mass constituency of working people and expand the New Deal legacy through programs such as universal health care, a federal living wage, new public works projects, revitalized collective bargaining rights, and tuition-free higher education, among other planks. Such programs would not only create a new floor of economic security after years of neoliberal austerity and privatization but would also crucially advance a durable and universalist conception of social welfare in which every American, regardless of race, is guaranteed the right to a decent living.

But particularly following Covid and the racial justice protests of 2020, progressives have also reacted to the increased economic pressures on working people by calling for explicitly race-targeted measures on the grounds that black Americans have suffered hardship disproportionately, both in the past and in the present. Some proponents of these policies have further insisted that restricting benefits to specific racial groups is the *only* appropriate solution to rectifying historical discrimination and addressing contemporary inequality: "The only remedy to racist discrimination is antiracist discrimination. The only remedy to past discrimination is present discrimination," Kendi has famously written.[26] By his account, policies that are race-neutral or universal are not only insufficient but even harmful because they don't explicitly account for accumulated past discrimination. "The most threatening racist movement is not the alt right's unlikely drive for a White ethnostate," Kendi has argued, "but the regular American's drive for a 'race-neutral' one."

As I discussed in the first chapter, this conception of justice has informed the Democratic Party's reckoning-era vision of racial equity, and after 2020, its leaders broadcast their commitment to the project in several ways. Biden, for instance, appointed more than 500 policy advisers with a mandate to "focus on race" in areas like housing and employment even prior to being sworn in.[27] Upon taking office, he further distinguished himself as the first American president to condemn "systemic racism" and "white supremacy" in his inaugural address and signed an executive order directing over ninety federal agencies to prioritize racial equity by dismantling "systemic barriers" and fighting racial disparities.[28] Blue states including California and cities such as New York soon followed suit with their own disparity-monitoring efforts, which included the establishment of special racial justice task forces to devise policies that would, in the words of former New York City mayor Bill De Blasio, "dismantle structural racism."[29]

Far more politically corrosive than these administrative gestures were a set of contentious race-targeted measures enacted during and after the racial reckoning. In the summer of 2020, at the height of the reckoning, Democratic lawmakers in Oregon approved a relief fund of $62 million targeted exclusively to black residents and business owners on the grounds that the state's long history of discrimination necessitated race-specific measures in the present. ("This is who needs the support right now," one legislator said.)[30] The measure earned the approval of the state's largest business lobbies, which released a joint statement applauding the decision.[31] "We recognize that the health and wellbeing of the entire Oregon business community is linked," the group said. "We also recognize that past and current racial discrimination have led to significant inequities, and those inequities are only growing due to the pandemic."

At the federal level, a stimulus bill the following year similarly allocated $4 billion in debt relief to "socially disadvantaged" farmers, explicitly defined in the legislation as non-white. Black farmers in particular, supporters noted, had historically suffered racist abuses such as Jim Crow–era land theft and the denial of Department of Agriculture loans that justified present debt relief. "For generations, socially disadvantaged farmers have struggled to fully succeed due to systemic discrimination and a cycle of debt," Agriculture Secretary Tom Vilsack said in a statement.[32]

Though both measures were applauded by racial justice advocates, they swiftly came under fire by others. The most immediate problem with attempting to ameliorate race-specific historic injustices during a pandemic that had shuttered businesses and put millions out of work, of course, was that people of all identities were suddenly and legitimately in need of support. Oregon was promptly sued for discrimination by three business owners (two white and another Mexican American) and nearly $9 million of the earmarked funds were frozen while the case went to court. The next year, the state reached settlements with the plaintiffs, which included issuing payouts to over 1,200 non-black applicants who had applied for grants but had been denied on the basis of their race. Meanwhile, white farmers in several states who were ineligible for the race-targeted federal debt relief also filed suit—some with the backing of right-wing groups like America First Legal—on the grounds that their exclusion from the program constituted racial discrimination. A few months into the court challenges, a federal judge halted the program's rollout; updated legislation the following year removed the controversial race-based criteria, expanding eligibility for debt relief to white farmers (who make up over 95 percent of farmers in the United States) while also reducing the available funding, watering down the aid significantly.

The legacy of these measures, then, has been an accumulation of legal bills and lingering resentment on all sides. While the initial race-based restrictions on the agricultural debt relief program had predictably infuriated struggling white farmers, the botched rollout in turn alienated black farmers who had been expecting aid only to find that none would be coming. "They gave us their word. We signed a contract and sent it back in and then they repealed the whole measure. I see it as a broken promise," John Boyd Jr., the president of National Black Farmers Association, said.[33] He and three other black farmers went on to file their own class-action lawsuit against the Biden administration for shuttering the program. In the lead-up to the 2024 election, other black farmers whose promised aid never materialized told the *New York Times* they were planning to punish the Democrats at the polls that year.[34] "I think we did better under President Trump," one such farmer in Georgia said.

For liberal commentators, the unraveling of the program was just more evidence of white hostility to black progress. "The argument made by white farmers suing over the USDA program is not a new one," one law professor wrote of the controversy.[35] "For more than a century, cynics and supremacists, intent on dividing and conquering to hold on to power, have propagated the false idea that conferring equality on nonwhite people amounts to discrimination against whites."

But the controversy over the race-targeted debt relief is less persuasive as an example of white supremacist power hoarding when considered in the context of a much larger farming crisis that had begun well before 2020. Starting in the 1980s, corporations had aggressively expanded into agriculture, resulting in a few giant agribusinesses holding near-monopolies on soybeans, corn, and livestock and pushing thousands of small farms into financial ruin. In the years before Covid, severe weather and ongoing trade disputes with Mexico and China had further exacerbated these already precarious conditions; a record number of family farms filed for bankruptcy in 2019. "The nation lost more than 100,000 farms between 2011 and 2018; 12,000 of those between 2017 and 2018 alone," *Time* magazine noted that year.[36] "Farm debt, at $416 billion, is at an all-time high." The pandemic sank American farms into even further distress by snarling supply chains, sending crop and livestock prices into freefall. According to the National Rural Health Association, the suicide rate for farmers in 2021 was 3.5 times greater than it was for other occupations due to sustained widespread financial insecurity and a lack of mental health resources.[37]

This is to say that one serious consequence of designing and pushing race-targeted aid based on historical injustices amid wider economic precarity is that it is a very difficult political sell for the constituencies that have suffered hardships that seem not to warrant the attention of Democrats and policy advisers fixated on racial equity. While such programs no doubt spring from a genuine desire to right past wrongs, this sort of particularism inevitably designates deserving victims (say, a black farmer who's fallen into debt because his father was denied a bank loan) and undeserving victims (say, a white farmer who's fallen into debt because he's struggling to compete with corporate farms). And not only does this narrow vision of justice reliably generate division and resentment, but it also serves to obscure—and even exonerate—the broader economic forces that have pushed an ever-increasing number of people of all races into distress.

Though the political pitfalls of what Kendi calls antiracist discrimination are perhaps especially pronounced after decades of trickle-down economics have threatened the financial stability of most working people, they were already apparent during a much earlier downturn. In a 1974 pamphlet titled "Affirmative Action in an Economy of Scarcity," Bayard Rustin and fellow civil rights organizer and labor leader Norman Hill cautioned against explicit systems of racial preference or racial quotas within the broader conditions of economic decline. "It seems painfully obvious that an affirmative action program cannot achieve its objectives peacefully and democratically if it must function within the context of scarcity," they noted.[38] "And we are particularly dismayed by the notion that opportunities can be expanded for some groups at a time when the job market is shrinking for all." While Rustin and Hill advocated the continuation of strong antidiscrimination measures in the labor market, they were equally adamant that such programs were "not the paramount reason for the economic gains" achieved by black Americans in the 1960s. The primary mechanisms for the advancement of blacks during that decade, they argued, had been low unemployment and antipoverty programs.

In fact, even prior to the passage of the Civil Rights Act in 1964—that is, even as the brutal Jim Crow regime was technically still in effect—black Americans, particularly those in the industrialized North, had benefited significantly from the postwar economic boom. Discrimination had no doubt stifled their advancement relative to whites during this period, but despite widespread racism, tight labor markets and high unionization rates had nonetheless delivered notable economic gains to black workers. The wage gap between black and white workers, for instance, fell by nearly 60 percent between 1940 and 1970, and the median income of black workers doubled between 1960 and 1970. Though affirmative action "certainly helped," Rustin and Hill noted, these gains primarily hadn't come about by "persuading a few corporations to hire additional black workers." Instead, they argued, the driving force had been "the availability of jobs, the growing opportunities for higher education, and all the other aspects of an expanding economy."

Today, however, Democrats' championing of racial equity at nearly every level of government tends to weaken their ambitions for the kind of broad-based economic reform that had once facilitated tremendous economic progress for black Americans. This runs the risk of creating an opening for a certain type of right-wing populism, particularly as public opinion on the country's economic prospects remains gloomy. In 2017, former Trump advisor Steve Bannon declared in an interview that the Democrats' preoccupation with race would be to Republicans' advantage.[39] "I want them to talk about racism every day," he said. "If the left is focused on race and identity, and we go with economic nationalism, we can crush the Democrats." In the years since, although Democrats have arguably sought to prioritize racial justice *and* simultaneously push for broader policies that strengthen the social safety net or the country's infrastructure, they've remained conspicuously weak-willed on the latter. In negotiations over the same federal stimulus bill that had contained the contentious race-targeted agricultural debt relief, for instance, congressional Democrats quickly folded on a provision to increase the federal minimum wage to $15 an hour. And the next year, when Bernie Sanders introduced a legislative amendment to reinstate the lapsed child tax credit, every single Democrat in the Senate voted against it. "Come on, Bernie," Ohio senator Sherrod Brown was overheard saying in exasperation.[40]

Likewise, though Covid had exacerbated and highlighted the inadequacy and cruelty of the United States' uniquely expensive and fragmented employer-based private health care system, in July of 2020, the Democratic Party rejected an amendment to include Medicare for All in its national platform. Following the summer's protests, Democrats and liberal commentators instead pivoted to a focus on racial disparities in Covid hospitalization and death rates. In Congress, Elizabeth Warren, Barbara Lee, and Ayanna Pressley introduced the Anti-Racism in Public Health Act, a bill to establish a new center within the Center for Disease Control that would not only track racial disparities in health outcomes but would also monitor police violence; a few months later, New York governor Kathy Hochul declared racism a public health crisis and signed an initiative to address medical racism and racial disparities in maternal health. Though a single-payer health care system would have almost certainly done more to address racial disparities in health outcomes than any of these specialized initiatives—and, by one estimate, could have prevented some 330,000 Covid deaths—the political momentum for such a program among Democratic lawmakers evaporated as the party turned its attention to the project of racial equity.[41]

The party's swift capitulation on measures like universal health care and a higher minimum wage—even as they continue to be extraordinarily popular among the Democratic base—has contrasted sharply with their enthusiasm for far more divisive initiatives. In the wake of 2020's reckoning, several of the country's most populous states, including California, Illinois, Pennsylvania, and New York, established task forces on reparations to black Americans for slavery. The California task force in particular has been the subject of much media coverage—liberal and conservative alike—and has publicly bandied about ideas like free college tuition for black students (though the cost of higher education for *all* students in the state has more than doubled since 2004) and up to $1.2 million in direct cash payments to descendants of slavery (though some 5 million Californians, the majority of whom are not black, live below the poverty line). Unsurprisingly, such proposals have struggled to gain support among the state's white, Hispanic, and Asian residents—who together make up over 90 percent of California's population—which suggests that any future reparations measures that are passed by the legislature will be vulnerable to the same legal challenges and electoral blowback that the other race-targeted measures rushed out after 2020 have faced. In a context of economic scarcity, so-called antiracist discrimination—even when intended as a response to very real historical injustices—is political poison.

Empty "Wages of Whiteness"

As the reckoning-era preoccupation with racial equity has continued to crowd out (or cast doubt upon) universal economic demands in progressive policy circles, some left-wing scholars and activists have tried to resolve this tension by insisting that centering race is a *precondition* for winning broader economic reforms because racism continues to divide what might otherwise be a united working-class front. "We will never be able to unify a multi-racial working class without confronting structural racism," reads the official political platform of the Democratic Socialists of America. In a 2021 podcast interview, law professor and author Ian Haney López similarly argued for the importance of foregrounding race in progressive political appeals. "I want to say this very clearly," he said.[42] "Racism against black and brown people is the *number one threat* in the lives of every American family, white families included."

The view that white workers' racism has perpetually fore-stalled the formation of a working-class movement in the US was first articulated by W. E. B. Du Bois in *Black Reconstruction*, in a passage that's arguably now the book's most famous: "It must be remembered that the white group of laborers, while they received a low wage, were compensated in part by a sort of public and psychological wage," Du Bois wrote. "They were given public deference and titles of courtesy because they were white. They were admitted freely with all classes of white people to public functions, public parks, and the best schools." Though it comprises just one short paragraph in a work more than 700 pages long, the passage has been invoked repeatedly over the decades and has inspired an entire body of scholarship now known as whiteness studies. Scholars in this discipline, such as Theodore Allen, David Roediger, and Noel Ignatiev, have expanded the notion of a white "psychological wage" to argue that white work-ers have been (and continue to be) more committed to the idea of their own racial superiority than they are to the possibility of economic advancement for all. Roediger's influential work *The Wages of Whiteness*, for instance, claimed that white workers weren't simply manipulated into animosity toward their black counterparts by bosses, but themselves harbored a deep and violent attachment to their racial identity. "A white identity has led to absences of humanity and of the effective pursuit of class interest among whites," he wrote.

The idea that white workers possess a kind of false conscious-ness—or white privilege—that continually stands in the way of social change continues to enthrall progressives; even those who readily acknowledge the dire conditions faced by the victims of deindustrialization, rural disinvestment, and deaths of despair have found ways to trace these predicaments back to working-class whites' supposed investment in the idea of their own racial superiority. In his acclaimed 2019 book *Dying of Whiteness: How the Politics of Racial Resentment is Killing America's Heartland*, author Jonathan Metzl argued that this misguided allegiance to whiteness had induced poor whites in red states to vote repeatedly against their "biological self-interests" by supporting lax gun laws, tax cuts for the rich, and antiwelfare measures. Though these and other Republican policies were making them poorer and sicker over the long run, he wrote, working-class whites were nevertheless willing to "put their own bodies on the line, rather than imagining scenarios in which diversity or equity might better the flourishing of everyone." According to Metzl, exiting this deadly cycle would ultimately require red state residents to "stop falling for the racist scapegoating" of politicians and instead support measures like expanded health care and increased social spending. "Can you imagine what would happen to the GOP agenda if working-class white communities in the South said, 'Yeah, we support the GOP, but we also want Medicaid expansion and we want better schools and bridges and we want the government to stop giving tax breaks to rich people'?" he asked in a 2019 interview.[43] "The minute that happens, the GOP agenda collapses."

Democratic commentators, of course, have been perpetually captivated—even sometimes delighted—by the idea that Republican policies end up hurting average Republican voters. ("Be happy for coal miners losing their health insurance. They're getting exactly what they voted for," went one infamous 2016 entry in the popular liberal outlet Daily Kos.)[44] But punishing as the GOP agenda may be, a closer look at red state politics doesn't support the claim that working-class whites in these areas constitute the main barrier to progressive reform. For instance, in 2018, a year before *Dying of Whiteness* was published, nearly two-thirds of the voters in Idaho—one of the most Republican states in the country, with a population more than 90 percent white—did exactly what Metzl would propose: They passed a ballot measure to expand Medicaid in the state despite vociferous opposition from Republican state legislators. This was no isolated incident; over the next five years, residents of several other Republican states, including Missouri, Utah, Nebraska, and South Dakota, also went on to approve ballot measures to expand Medicaid in those states. These measures, according to *Politico*, constituted "the most significant growth of Medicaid expansion since the early phase of the Affordable Care Act—and a resounding rebuke to GOP lawmakers in states that have rejected a program that's financed mostly with federal dollars."[45]

And against the idea that any meaningful political change in red states would first require a serious reckoning with whiteness—an embrace of "white humility," as Metzl put it—the Trump-country Medicaid expansions had taken place as the result of a process far more mundane than any kind of widespread soul-searching or meditation on racism. In Idaho, a nonpartisan group of volunteers simply knocked on doors—first to collect the signatures needed to place the expansion on the ballot and then again to urge voters to vote yes on the measure. "If we do our work of going out and finding our supporters, getting our message across, we will win," organizer Luke Mayville told one local news station.[46] In 2019, voters in deep-red Nebraska likewise circumvented hostile Republican legislators to win a higher minimum wage through a ballot initiative; the next year they repeated the process to win paid sick leave, a proposal that had died with legislators multiple times before.

But despite Metzl's prediction, the GOP agenda in these states has not collapsed as a result of white residents expressing their preferences for measures like expanded Medicaid or a higher minimum wage at the ballot box. Instead, Republican politicians have responded to these popular mandates by attempting to ignore or override them in order to push their favored brand of austerity politics. The GOP legislators of Idaho and Utah have tried year after year to repeal the Medicaid expansions approved by their voters (and, when unable to do so, have settled for undermining the programs by instituting onerous work requirements and other administrative hurdles). In Missouri, after residents approved a Medicaid expansion in 2020, lawmakers simply left the program out of the state's annual budget until forced by the courts to include it.[47]

In other words, while whites who would rather die than support government programs that might also help non-whites do still exist (and feature prominently in Metzl's book and whiteness studies texts), this group of people simply does not constitute the majority of working-class whites, nor do they exert more sway over American politics than, say, Republican lawmakers, business lobbies like the Chamber of Commerce, or Charles Koch personally. As political scientist Cedric Johnson has noted, the argument that white workers by default possess a self-defeating investment in white supremacy not only can't account for the many instances of successful interracial organizing that have occurred even during the nation's most reactionary periods but also wrongly "presupposes that racial identity is the foremost shaper of working-class thought and action."[48]

It's furthermore only possible to sustain the argument that white workers' racial prejudices are today the driving force behind the disorganization of the working class by ignoring or downplaying the many ruling-class assaults on working-class institutions throughout the twentieth and twenty-first centuries. These include not only the perennial efforts by business interests to smash unions and roll back any labor laws or government regulations that threaten to cut into their profits but also the steady erosion of democracy through the presence of big money in politics; the disappearance of public spaces and civic organizations as the result of rampant privatization; and a rural-urban divide that continues to grow sharper and sharper, spurred not least by a stream of self-satisfied liberal condemnations of the non-coastal non-elite, such as 2024's *White Rural Rage*, which posits that aggrieved whites in flyover country currently pose the greatest threat to the US. All these developments have exacerbated a harrowing increase in social isolation among Americans that has, in turn, depressed political participation and cratered the public's trust in government. Though historically, racial prejudice has certainly played some role in undermining what we might understand as class solidarity, the idea that it is, as Theodore Allen once wrote, "the No. 1 barrier to the development of a class conscious-ness movement" is at best a misapprehension of the balance of political power in the US, especially today, and at worst a type of antipopulism that conceives of non-Hispanic white workers—still over 63 percent of the population—as bigoted dupes that progressives should have no problem writing off.

The Racial Justice Vanguard

The same antipopulism that imagines a significant portion of the public as backwards or narrow-minded on matters of race naturally also demands a class of professional racial justice experts to oversee antiracist education for the masses. Today this includes not only the for-profit DEI industry but also an expansive informal network of nonprofits, think tanks, academics, and other policy specialists concerned broadly with the administration of racial equity in society. Though these groups frequently profess to represent the marginalized, in the twenty-first century most function not as mass member-ship organizations that directly mobilize constituencies but as elite pressure groups that influence public policy through their access to lawmakers, wealthy donors, and the legacy media.

When it comes to the subject of race and racism, this elite-driven advocacy has often taken the form of an explicit vanguardism that envisions the public as a stubborn obsta-cle to social change. In 2021, for instance, the left-leaning Roosevelt Institute released a seventy-three-page policy report on the legacy of racial inequality in the US that argued that

Americans needed expert guidance on matters of race in the wake of 2020's racial justice demonstrations and the subsequent right-wing backlash. "To lead a recalcitrant and divided public, and to make a new policy approach possible, we need a new paradigm—meaning a new, broadly held common sense for what racial justice requires," the authors declared.[49] In an accompanying article for the influential liberal policy journal *Democracy*, they added, "Public opinion in this country has never been the place to start on matters of racial justice, because it has never been race-forward," noting that nearly 70 percent of voters in 1964 had been "hesitant about the newly passed Civil Rights Act and wanted to see it enforced moderately."[50] According to the authors, it was instead the task of "movement actors"—identified as "scholars, public intellectuals, activists, and historians"—to forge a consensus on race that could guide average citizens.

One can, of course, unearth any number of illiberal racial attitudes from the middle of the last century. But it's also the case that in 1964, despite the ambivalence around its implementation, nearly 60 percent of Americans—a population that was at the time around 85 percent white—nevertheless said they supported the Civil Rights Act.[51] By the next year, 76 percent supported the Voting Rights Act. The point is not that racism during this era was not a serious problem—very clearly it was—but rather that in any putative democracy, public opinion is no less useful a place to start, so to speak, than the preferences or sensibilities of think tank and nonprofit leaders. Public opinion that diverges from the consensus of "movement actors" can furthermore occasionally illuminate useful distinctions. A 2023 Pew survey, for instance, found that two-thirds of the public thought that Black Lives Matter had been successful at "bringing attention to racism against Black people."[52] But a majority of respondents also said they believed that the movement hadn't done much to improve the lives of most black people, which is difficult to dispute in light of the fact that rates of police violence or the number of black Americans living in poverty haven't changed much since either the inception of the movement or 2020's moment of national reckoning. That suggests that for all the handwringing within certain policy circles, the supposedly "recalcitrant" public appears to understand the phenomenon of Black Lives Matter better than those who have appointed themselves the task of guiding the masses to a new state of racial awareness.

But for think tanks, academic specialists, progressive media outlets, and even grassroots nonprofits, the idea of a citizenry possessed of reactionary attitudes is alluring because it secures the aforementioned experts an important—even permanent—leadership role in the management of society. The solution to the problem of a general public that fails to understand or acknowledge the importance of race is the kind of consciousness raising that comes in the form of white papers on systemic racism from think tanks, antiracism seminars conducted by consultants and nonprofits, and articles and books unearthing the latest variants of racism previously unknown to the public. (Recent titles in this vein include *Colorblind Racism*, *Nice Racism*, and *Metaracism*, among others.) This also explains why so many of those invested in a vanguardist approach to social change often discuss racism as a kind of chronic, incurable illness that can never be eliminated, only treated with the correct regimen. (Robin DiAngelo, for instance, claims on her consulting website, "Racism must be continually identified, analyzed and challenged; no one is ever done," while Kendi has compared antiracist education to fighting an addiction and has proposed that the government establish a Department of Antiracism to perform this task on a federal level.) Just as DEI consultants' paychecks depend not *quite* on eradicating racism—but, rather, on identifying and managing it—the racial equity intelligentsia, no matter how pure their personal motives, have professional and financial incentives to ensure that race remains the country's most pressing division.

This consciousness-raising approach has also encouraged the proliferation of what Cedric Johnson has called "public therapy," a hollow form of politics that elevates individual acts of self-improvement or atonement as the basis of wide-scale social transformation.[53] At the height of 2020's protests, this memorably took the form of affluent whites engaging in bizarre acts of self-flagellation or charity, such as sending money via Venmo and other apps to black friends and strangers alike as a type of peer-to-peer reparations.[54] ("Reparations must be ongoing and interpersonal," read an Instagram graphic shared by the writer and director Lena Dunham that summer.)[55] In an even more extreme version of the practice, several white homeowners in Portland, Oregon, sold their houses at losses of hundreds of thousands of dollars to black people as a way of, in the words of NPR, "taking reparations into their own hands."[56] (Selling to some racial groups but not others technically violates the 1968 Fair Housing Act; luckily, the individuals involved were able to circumvent that particular civil rights law by working with a special group that facilitates private sales between guilt-stricken homeowners and their chosen beneficiaries.) As Johnson notes, there is a "millenarian and liberal individualist dimension" to this kind of practice, which ultimately thwarts genuine collective action. "We are told individuals must correct their flaws before they can participate with others, a view that runs counter to what should be conventional wisdom about human behavior and social movement dynamics," he writes. Another word for this kind of public soul-searching, of course, is *reckoning*.

CONCLUSION
AFTER THE NEOLIBERAL CONSENSUS

Since the summer of 2020, progressives have continually attempted to explain away the explicit ruling-class enthusiasm for antiracism by dismissing it as a "co-optation" or a watering-down of a more genuine or radical form of racial justice. What I've tried to show in these chapters, however, is that the entanglement of antiracist ideology and capitalist power in the twenty-first century goes far beyond nefarious corporations and politicians perverting grassroots activist demands. At the very least, antiracism is an ideology that mystifies or misidentifies the sources of present-day economic precarity; at its worst, it legitimates the current regime of inequality and enables cynical (or simply misguided) adherents to discount or even suppress universalist social-democratic reforms even though such policies time and again have proven more effective at reducing and eliminating racial disparities than divisive race-targeted programs.

A more egalitarian society hasn't been—and won't be—inaugurated by a national reckoning on race and all the corporate money, professional-class vanguardism, and solipsistic public therapy that such a moment inevitably attracts. Rather, this future will only be won through the comparatively plain work of building a mass movement capable of demanding and winning an economy and a government that operates on behalf of all Americans who work for a living rather than on behalf of the wealthy few. This was the promise of the sweeping working-class victories of the last century—the New Deal and the Civil Rights Movement—which were ambitious experiments that profoundly altered the country for the better even as they have remained unfinished. And any effort to assemble a new majoritarian project in this mold necessarily requires a degree of faith in the public that looks less like the top-down "racial justice paradigms" proffered by think tanks in the wake of 2020 and more like the approach of the late Labor Party founder and union leader Tony Mazzocchi, who used to remind other party members of the importance of beginning with rank-and-file constituents rather than administering decrees from above by saying, "If you can't get it passed in your own union hall, don't bring it to a broader organization."[1]

Today the neoliberal consensus that ruled American political life for nearly half a century has been broken and a growing number of mainstream politicians and pundits have openly acknowledged its disastrous consequences for the working class. Upon taking office in 2021, Biden repeatedly expressed support for labor organizing, investment in infrastructure, and the revival of American manufacturing, while members of his administration signaled their rejection of free market worship by calling for a "new economic world order" and an end to the "Washington consensus." By the end of his term, however, Biden's ambitions for a fairer economy had largely fallen short. Unlike former Mexican president Andrés Manuel López Obrador to the south—who had won a critical mass of working-class constituents to his party by campaigning on economic populism and successfully retained their loyalty by making the government work for them—Bidenomics floundered amid record inflation, half-fulfilled infrastructure projects, and, yes, the distraction of a Democratic Party that, for at least a time, eagerly attached itself to activist antiracist rhetoric and a battery of unpopular and counterproductive racial equity policies that the right swiftly pounced upon.

Though neoliberalism may be in its death throes, American workers won't benefit from its decline absent a robust, well-organized political movement for a just economy. And antiracism in the twenty-first century—as an ideology that has been wholeheartedly embraced by the class that benefits most from the present unequal economic order—impedes this effort rather than facilitating or complementing it. "As long as inequality is treated as the product of racism, instead of economics, it will seriously divert the attention of society from difficult issues which ultimately must be faced," Bayard Rustin and Norman Hill had warned in 1974. Five decades on—with the rich inclined toward the project of antiracism as never before—this predicament has only sharpened.

The point, of course, is not that the rich alone possess an affinity for antiracism. From the explosive street protests to the internal convulsions that overtook America's most elite institutions, the 2020 racial reckoning fundamentally represented a *cross-class* demand to end racial disparities in American life. But the fact that the reckoning was able to accommodate a multitude of sentiments expressed by a variety of class interests—ranging from the call to end police violence to the call to increase the number of black-owned brands on the shelves at major retailers—was precisely the problem. Any movement with a fighting chance of refashioning a radically unjust economic order that has consigned the vast majority of people of all races to increasing insecurity will necessarily have to oppose the class that's not only deeply invested in the preservation of that order but incredibly adept at leveraging antiracism to that very end.

ACKNOWLEDGMENTS

Thanks to everyone at Verso who made this possible, particularly Asher Dupuy-Spencer and Ariella Thornhill, who championed the project from the start and supplied many thoughtful suggestions and edits along the way.

Thanks to Adolph Reed Jr., Touré Reed, and Walter Benn Michaels for their generous advice and for modeling conviction; to Catherine Liu, Vivek Chibber, Cedric Johnson, Bhaskar Sunkara, and Katherine Isaac for their insights and encouragement; to Amber Frost, Dustin Guastella, Ben Fong, and Katie Rader for crucial conversations on chapters; and to Sam Ross, Amanda Ufheil-Somers, Neima Jahromi, and Natalie Peart for keeping me in good humor from afar.

Thanks to my family—immediate, extended, and in-law—for their love and optimism throughout this process.

Thanks, most of all, to Frank. Slavoj Žižek once said, "Today passionate engagement is considered almost pathological. I think there is something subversive in saying: This is the man or woman with whom I want to stake everything." I agree.

NOTES

Introduction

1 Peter J. Kellogg, "Civil Rights Consciousness in the 1940s," *The Historian* 42, no. 1 (1979), 29.

2 Larry Buchanan, Quoctrung Bui, and Jugal K. Patel, "Black Lives Matter May Be the Largest Movement in U.S. History," *New York Times*, July 3, 2020, nytimes.com.

3 Emily Jacobs, "Mitch McConnell Denounces Officers in George Floyd Case, Calls for Justice," *New York Post*, June 2, 2020, nypost.com.

4 Maurice Mitchell, "Announcing the WFP Justice Fund," fundraising email, July 13, 2020.

5 Sharon Epperson and Lindsey Jacobson, "$340 Billion Pledged by Companies to Support Racial Equity Following George Floyd's Murder: McKinsey," CNBC, January 21, 2023, cnbc.com.

6 Thomas B. Edsall, "The Law of Unintended Political Consequences Strikes Again," *New York Times*, January 5, 2022, nytimes.com; Emmanuel Felton, "Open Society Foundations Announces Grants to Help Black Activists Make Their Work More Sustainable," *Washington Post*, February 4, 2022, washingtonpost.com.

7 MacKenzie Scott, "116 Organizations Driving Change," *Medium*, July 28, 2020, medium.com.

8 Nicole Aschoff, *The New Prophets of Capital* (Verso, 2015), 3.

9 Judith Stein, *Running Steel, Running America: Race, Economic Policy, and the Decline of Liberalism* (University of North Carolina Press, 1998), 151.

1. The Road to Reckoning

1 Gushers (@gushers), Twitter, June 5, 2020.

2 Ian Zelaya, "Uber Urges Those Who Tolerate Racism to Delete the App," *Adweek*, August 28, 2020, adweek.com.

3 Sundar Pichai, "Our Commitments to Racial Equity," *Keyword* (blog), June 17, 2020, blog.google.

4 Amazon (@amazon), Twitter, May 31, 2020.

5 Sydney Ember, "Bernie Sanders Predicted Revolution, Just Not This One," *New York Times*, June 19, 2020, nytimes.com.

6 Dealbook, "Corporate America's Role in the Fight for Racial Justice," *New York Times*, October 1, 2020, nytimes.com.

7 Doug McMillon, "Walmart CEO: Business Roundtable Members Have New Plans to Fight Historic Racial Injustice," *USA Today*, October 15, 2020, usatoday.com.

8 "Racial Equity and Justice Initiative: Year One Update," Business Roundtable, 2021, businessroundtable.org; "Our $30 Billion Racial Equity Commitment," Chase, 2023, jpmorganchase.com.

9 "Big Business," Gallup, news.gallup.com.

10 Ben Schiller, "Americans Agree on Something: They Don't Like Big Corporations," *Fast Company*, November 15, 2017, fastcompany.com.

11 Justin McCarthy, "U.S. Approval of Interracial Marriage at New High of 94%," Gallup, September 10, 2021, news.gallup.com.

12 Gary Gerstle, *The Rise and Fall of the Neoliberal Order* (Oxford University Press, 2022), 13.

13 Ibid.

14 Nancy Fraser, "From Progressive Neoliberalism to Trump—and Beyond," *American Affairs* 1, no. 4 (2017), americanaffairsjournal.org.

15 Tess Thorman, Daniel Payares-Montoya, and Joseph Herrera, "Income Inequality in California," Public Policy Institute of California fact sheet, March 2023, ppic.org; Morgan Keith, "California Has the Highest Poverty Level of All States in the US, According to US Census Bureau Data," *Business Insider*, September 14, 2021, businessinsider.com.

16 Dylan Riley, "Faultlines," *New Left Review* 126 (2020), newleftreview.org.

17 Nick Hanauer and David M. Rolf, "The Top 1% of Americans Have Taken $50 Trillion from the Bottom 90%—And That's Made the U.S. Less Secure," *Time*, September 14, 2020, time.com.

18 Estelle Sommeiller, Mark Price, and Ellis Wazeter, *Income Inequality in the U.S. by State, Metropolitan Area, and County* (Economic Policy Institute, June 16, 2016), epi.org.

19 Juliana Kaplan, "Workers Lost $3.7 Trillion in Earnings during the Pandemic. Women and Gen Z Saw the Biggest Losses," *Business Insider*, January 25, 2021, businessinsider.com.

20 Simone Silvan, "Almost 20% of U.S. Households Lost Entire Savings during Covid," Bloomberg, October 13, 2021, bloomberg.com.

21 Anna Cooban, "Billionaires Added $5 Trillion to Their Fortunes during the Pandemic," CNN, January 16, 2022, cnn.com.

22 Cedric Johnson, "Don't Let Blackwashing Save the Investor Class," *Jacobin*, June 24, 2020, jacobinmag.com.

23 Gerstle, *Rise and Fall of the Neoliberal Order*, 291.

24 "Business Roundtable Redefines the Purpose of a Corporation to Promote 'an Economy That Serves All Americans,'" Business Roundtable press release, August 19, 2019, businessroundtable.org.

25 Ibid.

26 Klaus Schwab, "Why We Need the 'Davos Manifesto' for a Better Kind of Capitalism," World Economic Forum, December 1, 2019, weforum.org.

27 Vivian Hunt, Bruce Simpson, and Yuito Yamada, "The Case for Stakeholder Capitalism," McKinsey, November 12, 2020, mckinsey.com.

28 Editors, "'Justice at the Necessary Scale': An Interview with Olúfẹ́mi Táíwò," *Drift*, January 26, 2020, thedriftmag.com.

29 William Lazonick, "Profits without Prosperity," *Harvard Business Review*, September 2014, hbr.org.

30 BBC Newsnight, "Firms Are 'Almost Eating Themselves' Andy Haldane Tells Newsnight," YouTube, July 25, 2015.

31 Kyle Bailey, "Stakeholder Capitalism against Democracy: Relegitimising Global Neoliberalism," *Journal of Australian Political Economy* 86 (2020), 89.

32 Rebecca M. Henderson, "Reimagining Capitalism in the Shadow of the Pandemic," *Harvard Business Review*, July 28, 2020, hbr.org.

33 "Bank of America Increases Commitment to Advance Racial Equality and Economic Opportunity to $1.25 Billion," Bank of America press release, March 30, 2021, newsroom.bankofamerica.com; Ken Klippenstein and Jon Schwarz, "Bank of America Memo, Revealed: 'We Hope' Conditions for American Workers Will Get Worse," *Intercept*, July 29, 2022, theintercept.com.

34 Rebecca Henderson, "Reimagining Capitalism," *MBR Journal*, Winter 2021, mbrjournal.com.

35 *Oversight of Federal Enforcement of the Antitrust Laws*, hearing before the US Senate Subcommittee on Competition Policy, Antitrust, and Consumer Rights of the US Senate Committee on the Judiciary, 117th Cong., September 20, 2022 (video), judiciary.senate.gov.

36 Karen Weise, "Jeff Bezos Commits $10 Billion to Address Climate Change," *New York Times*, February 17, 2020, nytimes.com.

37 Sophie Alexander, Szu Yu Chen, and Shera Avi-Yonah, "MacKenzie Scott's Money Bombs Are Single Handedly Reshaping America," Bloomberg, August 12, 2021, bloomberg.com.

38 Carl Rhodes, *Woke Capitalism: How Corporate Morality Is Sabotaging Democracy* (Bristol University Press, 2022), 70.

39 Silla Brush and Bill Allison, "BlackRock Spends Record on US Political Campaigns as ESG Fight Intensifies," Bloomberg, November 4, 2022, bloomberg.com.

40 Chuck Schumer, "Republicans Ought to Be All for ESG," *Wall Street Journal*, February 28, 2023, wsj.com.

41 Chris Kahn, "Many Republican Voters Agree with Biden—'Trickle-Down Economics' Has Failed," Reuters, April 29, 2021, reuters.com.

42 Ishan Desai-Geller, "When Did the Ruling Class Get Woke?" *Nation*, May 9, 2022, thenation.com.

43 Matthew J. Belvedere, "BET Founder Robert Johnson Calls for $14 Trillion of Reparations for Slavery," CNBC, June 1, 2020, cnbc.com; Beatrice Peterson, "Rep. Cori Bush Says $14 Trillion Reparations Bill Will 'Eliminate the Racial Wealth Gap,'" ABC News, May 19, 2023, abcnews.go.com.

44 Jessica DiNapoli, "U.S. Companies Should Consider Slavery Reparations, Vista Equity CEO Says," Reuters, August 12, 2020, reuters.com.

45 Maia Spoto and Kimberly Robinson, "Google, Apple Back Affirmative Action in Harvard Case," Bloomberg, August 1, 2022, bloomberg.com.

46 "Historic Number of Corporations File Amicus Briefs in U.S. Supreme Court in Support of College Admissions Policies That Foster Diversity," Legal Defense Fund press release, August 1, 2022, naacpldf.org.

47 Ibram X. Kendi, *How to Be an Antiracist* (One World, 2019), 14.

48 Walter Benn Michaels and Adolph Reed Jr., *No Politics but Class Politics* (ERIS, 2022), 342.

49 Max Abelson and Jordyn Holman, "A Wall Street Lifer's Quixotic Quest to Build a Nonracist Bank," Bloomberg, March 16, 2022, bloomberg.com.

50 "Our Story," Percapita, 2022, percapita.com.

51 Jeff Green et al., "Corporate America Promised to Hire a Lot More People of Color. It Actually Did," Bloomberg, September 25, 2023, bloomberg.com.

52 The Hill, "NEW AD: Kamala Harris Explores Difference between Equality and Equity in New 2020 Campaign Video," YouTube, November 1, 2020.

53 "Equity vs. Equality: What's the Difference?," San Diego Foundation, May 21, 2021, sdfoundation.org.

54 Nick Gass, "Clinton Knocks Sanders' College Plan: Trump's Kids Shouldn't Get Free Ride," *Politico*, October 5, 2015, politico.com.

55 Jacobin, "Why Liberals Make Everything about Race w/ Touré Reed | Jacobin Show," YouTube, March 10, 2021.

56 Bayard Rustin, "From Protest to Politics: The Future of the Civil Rights Movement," *Commentary*, February 1965, commentary.org.

57 Judith Stein, *Running Steel, Running America: Race, Economic Policy, and the Decline of Liberalism* (University of North Carolina Press, 1998), 195.

2. How Antiracism Became a Gift to Bosses

1 Diego Areas Munhoz, "NLRB Funding Boost Falls Short of White House, Unions' Requests," Bloomberg Law, December 21, 2022, bloomberglaw.com.

2 "With Global Spending Projected to Reach $15.4 Billion by 2026, Diversity, Equity & Inclusion Takes the Lead Role in the Creation of Stronger Businesses," Global Industry Analysts Inc. press release, November 3, 2021, prnewswire.com.

3 Jeff Green, "Corporate America Goes on a Diversity Officer Hiring Spree," Bloomberg, March 10, 2021, bloomberg.com.

4 Scripps National News, "Anti-racism Training Organizations Seeing Big Increase in Inquiries," YouTube, July 14, 2020.

5 Nick Niedzwiadek, "Blinken Names State Department's Chief Diversity and Inclusion Officer," *Politico*, April 12, 2021, politico.com; Jennifer Steinhauer, "As Military Addresses Diversity, Republicans See Culture War Target," *New York Times*, June 10, 2021, nytimes.com.

6   Schams Elwazer, "Royals Say They May Consider Appointing Diversity Chief," CNN, March 21, 2021, cnn.com.

7   Frank Dobbin and Alexandra Kalev, "Why Doesn't Diversity Training Work?," *Anthropology Now* 10, no. 2 (September 2018), 48.

8   Frank Dobbin and Alexandra Kalev, "Why Diversity Programs Fail," *Harvard Business Review*, July–August 2016, hbr.org.

9   Patrica G. Devine et al., "Long-Term Reduction in Implicit Race Bias: A Prejudice Habit-Breaking Intervention," *Journal of Experimental Social Psychology* 48, no. 6 (November 2012).

10 Frank Dobbin, *Inventing Equal Opportunity* (Princeton University Press, 2009), 4.

11 Judith Stein, *Running Steel, Running America: Race, Economic Policy, and the Decline of Liberalism* (University of North Carolina Press, 1998), 78.

12 Dobbin, *Inventing Equal Opportunity*, 220.

13 Ibid., 138.

14 Gary Stanley Becker, *The Economics of Discrimination* (University of Chicago Press, 1957).

15 "Diversity, Equity, and Inclusion," US Chamber of Commerce, 2023, uschamber.com; "Advancing Diversity, Equity, and Inclusion," Business Roundtable, 2023, businessroundtable.org; "World Economic Forum Launches Coalition to Tackle Racism in the Workplace," World Economic Forum, press release, January 25, 2021, weforum. org.

16 "What Is Diversity, Equity, and Inclusion?," McKinsey, August 17, 2022, mckinsey.com.

17 Drew Goldstein et al., "Unlocking the Potential of Chief Diversity Officers," McKinsey, November 18, 2022, mckinsey.com.

18 Frank Dobbin and Alexandra Kalev, *Getting to Diversity: What Works and What Doesn't* (Harvard University Press, 2022), 13.

19 Jeff Green, Katherine Chiglinsky, and Cedric Sam, "America's Top Employers Are Winning at Race Data Transparency—Except Musk and Buffett," Bloomberg, March 21, 2022, bloomberg.com.

20 "Diversity, Equity, Inclusion: New York Times Employee Recommendation Memo," NewsGuild of New York Local 31003, July 31, 2020, nyguild.org.

21 Kiara Alfonseca and Max Zahn, "How Corporate America Is Slashing DEI Workers amid Backlash to Diversity Programs," ABC News, July 7, 2023, abcnews.go.com.

22 Rachel Minkin, "Diversity, Equity and Inclusion in the Workplace," Pew Research Center, May 17, 2023, pewresearch.org.

23 Walt Disney Company, "Allyship for Race Consciousness," training document, 2021.

24 Frank Dobbin and Alexandra Kalev, "Why Diversity Programs Fail," *Harvard Business Review*, July–August 2016, hbr.org.

25 Brady Dennis, "Bank of America to Pay $335M to Settle Claims of Unfair Loans," *Washington Post*, December 21, 2011, washingtonpost.com.

26 Ryan Cooper and Matt Bruenig, "Destruction of Black Wealth during the Obama Presidency," People's Policy Project, December 7, 2017, peoplespolicyproject.org.

27 "Over 13,000 People Take Part in Racial Equity 21-Day Challenge," *Independent Tribune*, January 21, 2021, independenttribune.com.

28 United Way of Central Carolinas, "Racial Equity 21-Day Daily Content," training document, 2021.

29 Bridget Read, "Doing the Work at Work," *Cut*, May 26, 2021, thecut.com.

30 Michael Powell, "Inside a Battle over Race, Class and Power at Smith College," *New York Times*, February 24, 2021, nytimes.com.

31 Ibid.

32 Jodi Shaw, "Shame & Conformity in Smith College Department of Res Life," YouTube, November 4, 2020.

33 Charles Creitz, "Jodi Shaw Speaks Out on Smith College Resignation after White Staff Dubbed Bigots in 'Eating while Black' Case," Fox News, June 28, 2021, foxnews.com.

34 Powell, "Inside a Battle over Race."

35 Elizabeth Anderson, *Private Government* (Princeton University Press, 2017).

36 Ibid., xix.

37 Ben Hecht, "Moving beyond Diversity toward Racial Equity," *Harvard Business Review*, June 16, 2020, hbr.org.

38 Mark R. Kramer, "The 10 Commitments Companies Must Make to Advance Racial Justice," *Harvard Business Review*, June 4, 2020, hbr.org.

39 Arne L. Kalleberg, *Precarious Lives: Job Insecurity and Well-Being in Rich Democracies* (Polity Press, 2018).

40 Hassan A. Kanu, "NLRB's GM Ruling Gives Employers More Slack to Punish Speech," Bloomberg Law, July 21, 2020, bloomberglaw.com.

41 "NLRB Modifies Standard for Addressing Offensive Outbursts in the Course of Protected Activity," National Labor Relations Board, press release, July 21, 2020, nlrb.gov.

42 Sean P. Redmond, "NLRB Gets It Wright on Abusive Behavior," US Chamber of Commerce, July 21, 2020, uschamber.com.

43 Neena Hagen, "Pitt's Spending on 'Union Avoidance' Law Firm Nears $3M," *Pitt News*, January 11, 2022, pittnews.com; Labor and Employment Group, "NLRB Adopts Wright-Line Standard in Deciding Whether Employee Outbursts Constitute Protected Activity," Ballard Spahr, July 22, 2020, ballardspahr.com.

44 Pete Levine, "Studies Find Unions Close Gender and Racial Pay Gaps," AFSCME, September 13, 2021, afscme.org.

45 Paul Frymer and Jacob M. Grumbach, "Labor Unions and White Racial Politics," *American Journal of Political Science* 65, no. 1 (January 2021), 225–40.

46 Julia Belluz, "Companies Like Starbucks Love Anti-bias Training. But It Doesn't Work—and May Backfire," *Vox*, May 29, 2018, vox.com.

47 Sabrina Eaton, "Sen. Sherrod Brown Rips Bank CEOs at Senate Hearing," cleveland.com, May 26, 2021.

48 Celine McNicholas et al., "Employers Spend More Than $400 Million per Year on 'Union-Avoidance' Consultants to Bolster Their Union-Busting Efforts," Economic Policy Institute, March 29, 2023, epi.org; Rachel Phua, "Companies Are Required to Report Their Union Busting, but Many Don't," *American Prospect*, September 5, 2022, prospect.org.

49 Lee Fang, "The Evolution of Union-Busting," *Intercept*, June 7, 2022, theintercept.com.

50 "When Diversity and Inclusion Become Union Issues," Projections, 2023, projectionsinc.com.

51 "Union Avoidance Ethics: How to Fight a Union with Zero Drama," Greer Consulting Inc., 2022, hiregci.com.

52 Natacha Catalino et al., "Effective Employee Resource Groups Are Key to Inclusion at Work. Here's How to Get Them Right," McKinsey, December 7, 2022, mckinsey.com.

53 "Employee Voice—The Key for Better Employee Engagement," Projections, 2023, projectionsinc.com.

54 E. Phileda Tennant, "Employees' Input on ESG May Reduce Risks of Unionization," Law360 Employment Authority, May 26, 2022, law360.com.

55 Michael R. Hatcher, Weldon H. Latham, and Felicia K. Marsh, "How Companies Can Best Benefit from Employee Resource Groups (ERGs)," Jackson Lewis, December 27, 2022, jacksonlewis.com.

56 Maxwell Tani, "MSNBC Brass Push Back against Staff Unionization Drive Despite Support from High-Profile Anchors," *Daily Beast*, June 18, 2021, thedailybeast.com.

57 Karen Weise and Noam Scheiber, "Why Amazon Workers Sided with the Company over a Union," *New York Times*, April 16, 2021, nytimes.com.

58 Dobbin and Kalev, *Getting to Diversity*, 10.

59 Jennifer Miller, "Why Some Companies Are Saying 'Diversity and Belonging' Instead of 'Diversity and Inclusion,'" *New York Times*, May 13, 2023, nytimes.com.

60 Tatyana Monnay, "Wall Street Firms Build Diversity Practices after Court Decision," Bloomberg Law, November 17, 2023, bloomberglaw .com.

61 Pamela Newkirk, *Diversity, Inc.: The Failed Promise of a Billion-Dollar Business* (Bold Type Books, 2019), 193.

62 Kim Tran, "The Diversity and Inclusion Industry Has Lost Its Way," *Harper's Bazaar*, March 23, 2021, harpersbazaar.com.

63 Greg Hills et al., "A CEO Blueprint for Racial Equity," FSG, July 7, 2020, fsg.org.

64 Hecht, "Moving beyond Diversity."

65 Foundation against Intolerance and Racism, "Racial Justice: The Next Frontier—Combined Clips 2–5," YouTube, March 8, 2023.

66 Amber Burton and Paolo Confino, "Wharton to Offer Diversity Major to Prepare Students for 'New Realities of Leadership,'" *Fortune*, October 25, 2022, fortune.com.

67 Taylor Telford and Julian Mark, "DEI Is Getting a New Name. Can It Dump the Political Baggage?," *Washington Post*, May 5, 2024, washingtonpost.com.

68 Taylor Nicole Rogers, "Is the Corporate DEI Panic Finally Over?," *Financial Times*, May 6, 2024, ft.com.

69 Paige McGlauflin and Trey Williams, "Microsoft, Salesforce, and Other Fortune 500 Companies React to Supreme Court Striking Down Affirmative Action: 'Our Commitment to Equality Doesn't Waver,'" *Fortune*, June 30, 2023, ft.com.

70 "Message to Starbucks Partners about Our Commitment to Equity and Opportunity," Starbucks Stories and News, June 30, 2023, stories .starbucks.com.

3. Class Dismissed

1 John Blake, "There Was No Racial Reckoning," CNN, May 25, 2021, cnn.com.

2 Ailsa Chang, Rachel Martin, and Eric Marrapodi, "Summer of Racial Reckoning," NPR, August 16, 2020, npr.org; Gene Demby et al., "The Racial Reckoning That Wasn't," NPR, June 9, 2021, npr.org.

3 Barbara Ehrenreich and John Ehrenreich, "The New Left: A Case Study in Professional- Managerial Class Radicalism," *Radical America* 11, no. 3 (May–June 1977).

4 Barbara Ehrenreich, *Fear of Falling* (HarperPerennial, 1989), 132.

5 Barbara Ehrenreich and John Ehrenreich, *Death of a Yuppie Dream* (Rosa Luxemburg Stiftung, 2013), 11.

6 Ibid.

7 Elaine Godfrey, "Thousands of Americans Have Become Socialists Since March," *Atlantic*, May 14, 2020, theatlantic.com.

8 Reed Richardson, "Journalism of, by and for the Elite," Fairness and Accuracy in Reporting, March 23, 2018, fair.org.

9 Daniel Kreiss, "The Social Identity of Journalists," *Journalism* 20, no. 1 (January 2019), 27–31.

10 Heather Long et al., "The Covid-19 Recession Is the Most Unequal in Modern U.S. History," *Washington Post*, September 30, 2020, washingtonpost.com.

11 Taylor Dafoe and Caroline Goldstein, "The George Floyd Protests Spurred Museums to Promise Change. Here's What They've Actually Done So Far," Artnet News, August 14, 2020, news.artnet.com.

12 Ben Smith, "He Redefined 'Racist.' Now He's Trying to Build a Newsroom," *New York Times*, March 21, 2021, nytimes.com; Justin Curto, "Everything to Know about the Media's Reckoning with Abuse of Power," *Vulture*, July 24, 2020, vulture.com; Rebecca Jennings, "The Racial Reckoning in Women's Media," *Vox*, June 11, 2020, vox.com; Ginia Bellafante, "WNYC Employees Demanded Diversity. They Got Another White Boss," *New York Times*, July 3, 2020, nytimes.com.

13 Andrea Wenzel, "The Philadelphia Inquirer Is Working to Transform Its Newsroom. Here's What It's Done in a Year," Poynter Institute, August 27, 2021, poynter.org.

14 Paul Farhi and Sarah Ellison, "Ignited by Public Protests, American Newsrooms Are Having Their Own Racial Reckoning," *Washington Post*, June 13, 2020, washingtonpost.com.

15 Scott C. Johnston, "Revolution Consumes New York's Elite Dalton School," *Wall Street Journal*, December 29, 2020, wsj.com; Michael Powell, "New York's Private Schools Tackle White Privilege. It Has Not Been Easy," *New York Times*, August 27, 2021, nytimes.com.

16 Erin Einhorn, "Inside the Vast National Experiment in Test-Optional College Admissions," NBC News, April 10, 2022, nbcnews.com.

17 "Public Statement by Ibram X. Kendi," Boston Coalition for Education Equity, October 21, 2020, bosedequity.org.

18 Ayana Archie, "Harvard Releases Report Detailing Its Ties to Slavery, Plans to Issue Reparations," NPR, April 27, 2022, npr.org.

19 Harry Styles (@Harry_Styles), Twitter, May 30, 2020.

20 Ehrenreich and Ehrenreich, "The New Left."

21 Eduardo Bonilla-Silva, "Rethinking Racism: Toward a Structural Interpretation," *American Sociological Review* 62, no. 3 (June 1997), 470.

22 Anne Case and Angus Deaton, "The Great Divide: Education, Despair, and Death," *Annual Review of Economics*, 2022, 1–22.

23 B. Rose Huber, "Life Expectancy Gap between Black and White Americans Closes Nearly 50% in 30 Years," Princeton School of Public and International Affairs, September 28, 2021, spia.princeton.edu.

24 Joel Achenbach and Dan Keating, "A New Divide in American Death," *Washington Post*, April 10, 2016, washingtonpost.com.

25 Anne Case and Angus Deaton, "Rising Morbidity and Mortality in Midlife among White Non-Hispanic Americans in the 21st Century," *PNAS* 112, no. 49 (November 2015), pnas.org.

26 Selena Simmons-Duffin, "'Live Free and Die?' The Sad State of U.S. Life Expectancy," NPR, March 25, 2023, npr.org.

27 Julia Belluz, "What the Dip in US Life Expectancy Is Really About: Inequality," *Vox*, November 30, 2018, vox.com.

28 Doug Irving, "What Would It Take to Close America's Black-White Wealth Gap?," RAND, May 9, 2023, rand.org.

29 Ta-Nehisi Coates, "The Case for Reparations," *Atlantic*, June 2014, theatlantic.com.

30 Matt Bruenig, "The Racial Wealth Gap Is About the Upper Classes," People's Policy Project, June 29, 2020, peoplespolicyproject.org.

31 Keith Humphreys and Ekow N. Yankah, "Prisons Are Getting Whiter. That's One Way Mass Incarceration Might End," *Washington Post*, February 26, 2021, washingtonpost.com.

32 Jacobin, "Did the 13th Amendment Enable Mass Incarceration?—Touré Reed," *For the Record*, YouTube, November 3, 2022.

33 Joseph Friedman, Helena Hansen, and Joseph P. Gone, "What Does the 'Deaths of Despair' Narrative Leave Out?," *U Magazine*, June 29, 2023, uclahealth.org.

34 Adolph Reed Jr., "'Let Me Go Get My Big White Man': The Clientelist Foundation of Contemporary Antiracist Politics," *nonsite.org*, May 11, 2022.

35 Kenneth P. Vogel and Sarah Wheaton, "Major Donors Consider Funding Black Lives Matter," *Politico*, November 13, 2015, politico.com.

36 Nolan D. McCaskill, "Sanders 'Humiliated' by Democrats' Failure to Connect with Working Class," *Politico*, November 14, 2016, politico.com.

37 Ta-Nehisi Coates, "The First White President," *Atlantic*, October 17, theatlantic.com.

38 CNN, "Krugman: Trump Support about Race, Not Economic Anxiety," YouTube, September 15, 2016.

39 Mehdi Hasan, "Time to Kill the Zombie Argument: Another Study Shows Trump Won Because of Racial Anxieties—Not Economic Distress," *Intercept*, September 18, 2018, theintercept.com.

40 Barry Bluestone, foreword to Jefferson Cowie and Joseph Heathcott, eds., *Beyond the Ruins: The Meanings of Deindustrialization* (Cornell University Press, 2003), 7.

41 Jeff Faux, "NAFTA, Twenty Years After: A Disaster," *HuffPost*, January 1, 2014, huffpost.com.

42 Jiwon Choi et al., "Local Economic and Political Effects of Trade Deals: Evidence from NAFTA," NBER working paper 29525, November 2021, nber.org.

43 Richard J. Martin, *Factory Towns: A 10-State Analysis of the Democratic Presidential Vote Decline in Working-Class Counties, 2012–2020* (American Family Voices and 21st Century Democrats, June 2022).

44 CNN, "Donald Trump and Bernie Sanders Sound Alike on Trade," YouTube, June 29, 2016.

45 Christian Parenti, "Listening to Trump," *nonsite.org*, November 17, 2016.

46 Andrew J. Cherlin, "White Working Class Support for Trump," *Contexts* 20, no. 2 (Spring 2021), 32.

47 Andrew J. Cherlin, "In the Shadow of Sparrows Point," working paper, October 2019, 12.

48 Cherlin, "White Working Class Support for Trump," 32.

49 Ibid., 35.

50 Pauli Murray, "The Right to Equal Opportunity in Employment," *California Law Review* 33, no. 3 (September 1945), 432.

51 Patrick Bayer and Kerwin Kofi Charles, "Divergent Paths: A New Perspective on Earnings Differences between Black and White Men since 1940," *Quarterly Journal of Economics* 133, no. 3 (August 2018), 1459–501; Eric D. Gould, "Torn Apart? The Impact of Manufacturing Employment Decline on Black and White Americans," IZA Institute of Labor Economics, June 2018, iza.org.

52 Dan Balz, "Racial Attitudes Shifted over the Past Decade, Leaving the Two Parties Further Apart Than Ever," *Washington Post*, November 13, 2021, washingtonpost.com.

53 Ehrenreich, *Fear of Falling*, 120.

54 Cathy Park Hong (@cathyparkhong), Twitter, November 4, 2020.

55 Frank Rich, "No Sympathy for the Hillbilly," *New York*, March 20, 2017, nymag.com.

56 Thomas B. Edsall, "The Closing of the Republican Mind," *New York Times*, July 13, 2017, nytimes.com.

57 Jazmin L. Brown-Iannuzzi et al., "Wealthy Whites and Poor Blacks: Implicit Associations between Racial Groups and Wealth Predict Explicit Opposition toward Helping the Poor," *Journal of Experimental Social Psychology* 82, May 2019.

58 Lee Drutman, "Donald Trump Will Dramatically Realign America's Political Parties," *Foreign Policy*, November 16, 2016, foreignpolicy.com.

59 Monica Potts, "Why Democratic Appeals to the 'Working Class' Are Unlikely to Work," FiveThirtyEight, July 6, 2022, fivethirtyeight.com.

60 Ruy Teixeira, "White College Graduates Are the Democrats' New BFF," *Liberal Patriot*, March 23, 2023, liberalpatriot.com.

61 Nate Cohn, "Poll Shows Tight Race for Control of Congress as Class Divide Widens," *New York Times*, July 13, 2022, nytimes.com.

62 Nate Cohn, "Consistent Signs of Erosion in Black and Hispanic Support for Biden," *New York Times*, September 5, 2023, nytimes.com.

63 Ruth Igielnik, Scott Keeter, and Hannah Hartig, "Behind Biden's 2020 Victory," Pew Research Center, June 30, 2021, pewresearch.org.

64 Weiyi Cai and Ford Fessenden, "Immigrant Neighborhoods Shifted Red as the Country Chose Blue," *New York Times*, December 20, 2020, nytimes.com.

65 Ruy Teixeira, "The Democrats' Nonwhite Working Class Problem," *Liberal Patriot*, December 22, 2020, liberalpatriot.com.

66   Jared Abbott, "The Working Class Has Left the Building," *Jacobin*, November 18, 2024, jacobinmag.com.

67   J. David Goodman, Edgar Sandoval, and Robert Gebeloff, "'An Earthquake' Along the Border: Trump Flipped Hispanic South Texas," *New York Times*, November 8, 2024, nytimes.com.

68   Matthew Karp, "The Breakup," *Nation*, February 19, 2024, thenation.com.

4. The Culture War Void

1   Beth Reinhard and Josh Dawsey, "How a Trump-Allied Group Fighting 'Anti-white Bigotry' Beats Biden in Court," *Washington Post*, December 12, 2022, washingtonpost.com.

2   Ibid.

3   Emily Birnbaum, "Trump Adviser Stephen Miller's Legal Group Rakes in $44 Million," Bloomberg, November 17, 2023, bloomberg.com.

4   Emily Mae Czachor, "'Florida Is Where Woke Goes to Die,' Gov. Ron DeSantis Says after Reelection Victory," CBS News, November 9, 2022, cbsnews.com.

5   Benjamin Wallace-Wells, "How a Conservative Activist Invented the Conflict Over Critical Race Theory," *New Yorker*, June 18, 2021, newyorker.com.

6   Daniel Schlozman and Sam Rosenfeld, "The Hollow Parties," in Frances E. Lee and Nolan McCarty, eds., *Can America Govern Itself?* (Cambridge University Press, 2019), 121.

7   Paul Heideman, "Behind the Republican Party Crack-Up," *Catalyst*, September 9, 2021, catalyst-journal.com.

8   Nate Cohn, "It's Not Reagan's Party Anymore," *New York Times*, August 10, 2023, nytimes.com.

9   Christopher Rufo, "Critical Race Theory Briefing Book," *Christopher F. Rufo* (blog), February 14, 2023, christopherrufo.com.

10   Alex Seitz-Wald, "In Virginia, Republicans See Education, Curriculum Fears as a Path to Victory," NBC News, October 17, 2021, nbcnews.com.

11   Christopher Rufo (@realchrisrufo), Twitter, March 15, 2021.

12   Rod Gramer, "Laying Siege to Idaho Education Isn't a Home-Grown War. It's Imported by Conflict Entrepreneurs," *Idaho Capital Sun*, April 21, 2022, idahocapitalsun.com.

13   Benjamin Wallace-Wells, "How a Conservative Activist Invented the

Conflict over Critical Race Theory," *New Yorker*, June 18, 2021, new yorker.com.

14 Richard Vanderford, "Florida's DeSantis Takes Aim at 'Woke Capital,'" *Wall Street Journal*, July 28, 2022, wsj.com.

15 Pete Schroeder, "Insight: How Republican-Led States Are Targeting Wall Street with 'Anti-woke' Laws," Reuters, July 6, 2022, reuters.com.

16 Niels Veldhuis and Jason Clemens, "Opinion: Stakeholder Capitalism and ESG's Road to Socialism," *Financial Post*, January 21, 2022, financialpost.com.

17 Zachary Petrizzo, "Fox News Host Mark Levin's Bestseller 'American Marxism': A Work of Staggering Ignorance," *Salon*, August 20, 2021, salon.com.

18 Stuart Jeffries, "Why Theodor Adorno and the Frankfurt School Failed to Change the World," *New Statesman*, August 18, 2021, newstatesman.com.

19 Alex Seitz-Wald and Scott Wong, "Conservatives Blame Silicon Valley Bank Collapse on 'Diversity' and 'Woke' Issues," NBC News, March 13, 2023, nbcnews.com; Matt Walsh (@mattwalshblog), "No, the argument is that prioritizing things like 'equity and inclusion' in the military has made us weak and ridiculous and given men like Putin the probably correct impression that they can do whatever they want," Twitter, February 24, 2022; Fabiola Cineas, "No, DEI Isn't Making Airplanes Fall Apart," *Vox*, January 25, 2024, vox.com; Joe Gould and Nahal Toosi, "Vance Sends a Wokeness Questionnaire to State Nominees," *Politico*, July 27, 2023, politico.com.

20 Jonathan Weisman, "Are G.O.P. Voters Tiring of the War on 'Wokeness'?," *New York Times*, August 6, 2023, nytimes.com.

21 Jamelle Bouie, "Democrats, You Can't Ignore the Culture Wars Any Longer," *New York Times*, April 22, 2022, nytimes.com.

22 Jamaal Bowman (@JamaalBowmanNY), Twitter, May 3, 2021.

23 Brandon Gillespie, "Alexandria Ocasio-Cortez Rails against CRT Opposition: Teachers Should Be 'Fluent in How to Dismantle Racism,'" Fox News, July 20, 2021, foxnews.com.

24 Virginia Chamlee, "Gavin Newsom Shares Photo of Himself Reading Banned Books to 'Figure Out What These States Are So Afraid Of,'" *People*, March 31, 2022, people.com.

25 Andrew Zhang, "Ron DeSantis vs. Gavin Newsom Showdown on Fox Drew Nearly 5M Viewers," *Politico*, December 1, 2023, politico.com.

26 Lara Korte, "Newsom: DeSantis Isn't Anti-woke, He's 'Anti-Black,'" *Politico*, December 14, 2023, politico.com.

27 Peter A. Hall, Georgina Evans, and Sung In Kim, *Political Change and*

Electoral Coalitions in Western Democracies (New York: Cambridge University Press, 2023), 24.

28 Gary Gerstle, *The Rise and Fall of the Neoliberal Order* (Oxford University Press, 2022), 15.

29 Hall, Evans, and Kim, *Political Change and Electoral Coalitions*, 24.

30 Ibid., 25

31 "Attitudes on Same-Sex Marriage: Public Opinion on Same-Sex Marriage," Pew Research Center, May 14, 2019, pewresearch.org; Ted Van Green, "Americans Overwhelmingly Say Marijuana Should Be Legal for Medical or Recreational Use," Pew Research Center, November 22, 2022, pew research.org.

32 Ruy Teixeira, "The Democrats' Hispanic Voter Problem: More Evidence from the 2020 Pew Validated Voter Survey," *Liberal Patriot*, October 7, 2021, liberalpatriot.com.

33 Mike Lux, "Winning Back the Factory Towns That Made Trumpism Possible," American Family Voices, June 6, 2022, americanfamilyvoices .org.

34 Jeffrey M. Jones, "U.S. Political Party Preferences Shifted Greatly During 2021," Gallup, January 17, 2022, news.gallup.com.

35 Mike Allen, "Record Number of Americans Say They're Politically Independent," *Axios*, April 17, 2023, axios.com.

36 Matt Stoller, "Democrats Can't Win until They Recognize How Bad Obama's Financial Policies Were," *Washington Post*, January 12, 2017, washingtonpost.com.

37 Christopher Ingraham, "About 100 Million People Couldn't Be Bothered to Vote This Year," *Washington Post*, November 12, 2016, washingtonpost.com.

38 Jan E. Leighley and Jonathan Nagler, *Who Votes Now? Demographics, Issues, Inequality, and Turnout in the United States* (Princeton University Press, 2014).

39 Asma Khalid, Don Gonyea, and Leila Fadel, "On the Sidelines of Democracy: Exploring Why So Many Americans Don't Vote," NPR, September 10, 2018, npr.org.

40 Sean McElwee, "Why Non-Voters Matter," *Atlantic*, September 15, 2015, theatlantic.com.

41 Mark Baldassare et al., "California's Exclusive Electorate: A New Look at Who Votes and Why It Matters," Public Policy Institute of California, September 2019, ppic.org.

42 "The Untold Story of American Non-Voters," Knight Foundation, February 18, 2020, knightfoundation.org.

43 Martin Gilens and Benjamin I. Page, "Testing Theories of American Politics: Elites, Interest Groups, and Average Citizens," *Perspectives on Politics* 12, no. 3 (2014), 564–81.

44 Jared Bernstein, "'Democracy in America?': An Interview with Authors Ben Page and Martin Gilens," *Washington Post*, January 23, 2018, washingtonpost.com.

45 Jonathan Swan, Maggie Haberman, and Shane Goldmacher, "Pence Looks toward 2024 Run, Using Reagan's Playbook, Not Trump's," *New York Times*, May 15, 2023, nytimes.com.

46 Patrick Ruffini, "The Emerging Working-Class Republican Majority," *Politico*, November 4, 2023, politico.com.

47 Benjamin Fearnow, "Josh Hawley Says Democrats Making American Workers 'Compete with Slave Labor,'" *Newsweek*, March 6, 2021, newsweek.com.

48 "Conservatives Should Ensure Workers a Seat at the Table," American Compass, September 6, 2020, americancompass.org.

49 Christopher Caldwell, "Can There Ever Be a Working-Class Republican Party?," *New Republic*, February 8, 2021, newrepublic.com.

50 "The New Conservative Voter," American Compass, September 27, 2023, americancompass.org.

51 J. C. Pan, "There Is No Such Thing as a Conservative Workers' Movement," *New Republic*, September 11, 2020, newrepublic.com.

52 Sohrab Ahmari, "I Was Wrong: The GOP Will Never Be the Party of the Working Class," *Newsweek*, August 14, 2023, newsweek.com.

53 Benjamin Y. Fong and Dustin Guastella, "The Siren Song of 'Pro-Worker' Conservatism," *Jacobin*, December 10, 2020, jacobin.com.

54 "Americans' Dismal Views of the Nation's Politics," Pew Research Center, September 19, 2023, pewresearch.org.

55 George Leef, "SCOTUS Finally Pulls the Plug on Legal Discrimination," *National Review*, July 3, 2023, nationalreview.com.

56 Christopher Rufo (@realchrisrufo), Twitter, June 29, 2023.

57 Riddhi Setty, "Stephen Miller's Legal Group Targets Macy's Diversity Policies," Bloomberg Law, November 21, 2023, bloomberglaw.com.

58 Emily Birnbaum, "Trump Allies Attack Corporate 'Bigotry' against White Men," Bloomberg, December 11, 2023, bloomberg.com.

59 Ryan P. Williams and Scott Yenor, "Why America's 'Anti-Discrimination' Regime Needs to Be Dismantled," *American Mind*, January 1, 2024, americanmind.org.

60 Frank Dobbin, *Inventing Equal Opportunity* (Princeton University Press, 2009), 4.

61 Ibid., 12.

62 Sean Captain, "Workers Win Only 1% of Federal Civil Rights Lawsuits at Trial," *Fast Company*, July 31, 2017, fastcompany.com.

63 Maryam Jameel and Joe Yerardi, "Despite Legal Protections, Most Workers Who Face Discrimination Are on Their Own," Center for Public Integrity, February 28, 2019, publicintegrity.org.

64 Cruz Fox and David Schleifer, *American Perspectives on Racism and Racial Justice: A Hidden Common Ground Report* (Public Agenda, 2023).

65 Justin McCarthy, "Post-Affirmative Action, Views on Admissions Differ by Race," Gallup, January 16, 2024, gallup.com.

66 Nikki Graf, "Most Americans Say Colleges Should Not Consider Race or Ethnicity in Admissions," Pew Research Center, February 25, 2019, pewresearch.org.

67 "Majority Leader Schumer Statement on Supreme Court Decision on Affirmative Action," Senate Democrats, press release, June 29, 2023, democrats.senate.gov; "Pressley Statement on Supreme Court's Affirmative Action Ruling," Congresswoman Ayanna Pressley, press release, June 29, 2023, pressley.house.gov.

68 Michael Powell and Ilana Marcus, "The Failed Affirmative Action Campaign That Shook Democrats," *New York Times*, June 11, 2023, nytimes.com.

69 Christopher Rufo, "A New Civil Rights Agenda," *Christopher F. Rufo* (blog), January 19, 2024, christopherrufo.com.

70 Powell and Marcus, "The Failed Affirmative Action Campaign."

5. The Retreat from the Universal

1 Emmarie Huetteman, "Senate Approves Bill to Combat Opioid Addiction Crisis," *New York Times*, July 13, 2016, nytimes.com.

2 For more examples, see Marie Gottschalk, "The Opioid Crisis: The War on Drugs Is Over; Long Live the War on Drugs," *Annual Review of Criminology* 6 (2023), 363–98.

3 PBS Newshour, "There Was No Wave of Compassion When Addicts Were Hooked on Crack," YouTube, March 29, 2016.

4 Josh Keller and Adam Pearce, "A Small Indiana County Sends More People to Prison Than San Francisco and Durham, N.C., Combined. Why?" *New York Times*, September 2, 2016, nytimes.com.

5 Gottschalk, "The Opioid Crisis."

6 Laura Barrón-López, Alex Thompson, and Theodoric Meyer, "Clyburn Doesn't Want Biden to Be Like FDR," *Politico*, April 13, 2021, politico.com; "Alexandria Ocasio-Cortez and the New Left," *Intercept*, March 9, 2019, theintercept.com.

7 Touré F. Reed, *Toward Freedom: The Case against Class Reductionism* (Verso, 2020).

8 Bryce Covert, "There's a Reason We Can't Have Nice Things," *New York Times*, July 21, 2022, nytimes.com.

9 Larry DeWitt, "The Decision to Exclude Agricultural and Domestic Workers from the 1935 Social Security Act," *Social Security Bulletin* 70, no. 4 (2010), ssa.gov.

10 The Late Show with Stephen Colbert, "Jon Stewart: The New Deal and GI Bill Explicitly Excluded Black People," YouTube, June 25, 2020.

11 Suzanne Mettler, *Soldiers to Citizens: The G.I. Bill and the Making of the Greatest Generation* (Oxford University Press, 2005).

12 Paul Prescod, "No, the GI Bill Did Not Make Racial Inequality Worse," *Jacobin*, April 1, 2023, jacobin.com.

13 David R. Henderson and Phillip W. Magness, "'The 1619 Project' on Hulu Vindicates Capitalism," *Wall Street Journal*, February 20, 2023, wsj.com.

14 Tory Newmyer, "The Racial Homeownership Gap Is Widening. New Rules Might Make It Worse," *Washington Post*, December 7, 2023, washingtonpost.com.

15 Angela Lang, Black Leaders Organizing for Communities message to the FDIC, October 10, 2023, available at fdic.gov.

16 David Dayen, "The Curious Partner in Big Banks' Drive to Weaken Capital Rules," *American Prospect*, November 29, 2023, prospect.org.

17 Lily Geismer, *Left Behind: The Democrats' Failed Attempt to Solve Inequality* (Public Affairs, 2022), 224.

18 Jo Becker, Sheryl Gay Stolberg, and Stephen Labaton, "White House Philosophy Stoked Mortgage Bonfire," *New York Times*, December 20, 2008, nytimes.com.

19　"New HUD Report Identifies Barriers to Minority Homeownership," HUD press release, June 17, 2002, archives.hud.org.

20　Preston H. Smith II, "Race and the Housing Question," *Catalyst*, Spring 2023, catalyst-journal.com.

21　Dan Balz, Scott Clement, and Emily Guskin, "Post-ABC Poll Finds a Deeply Pessimistic Nation, Worried about the Economy and Biden's Leadership," *Washington Post*, February 27, 2022, washingtonpost.com.

22　Paul Krugman, "America's Very Peculiar Economic Funk," *New York Times*, March 3, 2022, nytimes.com.

23　Heather Cox Richardson (@HC_Richardson), Twitter, February 27, 2022.

24　Reade Pickert and Jennah Haque, "Just How Bad Is the US Cost-of-Living Squeeze? We Did the Math," Bloomberg, November 27, 2023, bloomberg.com.

25　Katherine G. Giefer, "Harder to Pay the Bills Now That Child Tax Credit Payments Have Ended," United States Census Bureau, February 28, 2022, census.gov.

26　Ibram X. Kendi, *How to Be an Antiracist* (One World, 2019).

27　Lananh Nguyen and Jennifer Epstein, "Biden Fills Economic Posts with Experts on Systemic Racism," Bloomberg, November 15, 2020, bloomberg.com.

28　Sarah Todd, "Joe Biden Is the First US President to Call Out White Supremacy in Inaugural Address," Quartz, January 20, 2021, qz.com.

29　Emma G. Fitzsimmons, "After Unrest and Protests, N.Y.C. Creates Group to Dismantle Structural Racism," *New York Times*, March 23, 2021, nytimes.com.

30　John Eligon, "A Covid-19 Relief Fund Was Only for Black Residents. Then Came the Lawsuits," *New York Times*, January 3, 2021, nytimes.com.

31　Matthew Kish, "Business Groups Announce Support for Fund That Supports Black Businesses, Oregonians," *Portland Business Journal*, December 9, 2020, bizjournals.com.

32　Laura Reiley, "Relief Bill Is Most Significant Legislation for Black Farmers since Civil Rights Act, Experts Say," *Washington Post*, March 8, 2021, washingtonpost.com.

33　Scott McFetridge, "Black Farmers Sue Government for Promised Federal Aid," PBS News, December 6, 2022, pbs.org.

34　Alan Rappeport, "Black Farmers in Georgia Cool to Biden, Reflecting a Bigger Challenge," *New York Times*, June 17, 2024, nytimes.com.

35 Sheryll Cashin, "Why a Debt Relief Program for Farmers Matters for Racial Equity in America," *Politico*, August 21, 2021, politico.com.

36 Alana Semuels, "'They're Trying to Wipe Us Off the Map.' Small American Farmers Are Nearing Extinction," *Time*, November 27, 2019, time.com.

37 Rosalie Eisenreich and Carolyn Pollari, "Addressing Higher Risk of Suicide among Farmers in Rural America," National Rural Health Association Policy Brief, February 2021, ruralhealth.us.

38 Bayard Rustin and Norman Hill, *Affirmative Action in an Economy of Scarcity*, testimony delivered by Norman Hill, September 17, 1974, to the Special Subcommittee on Education, US House of Representatives (A. Philip Randolph Institute, 1974).

39 Robert Kuttner, "Steve Bannon, Unrepentant," *American Prospect*, August 16, 2017, prospect.org.

40 Aris Folley and Mychael Schnell, "'Come On, Bernie': Democrats Clash on Senate Floor over Sanders Proposal," *Hill*, August 8, 2022, thehill.com.

41 Rachel Nuwer, "Universal Health Care Could Have Saved More Than 330,000 U.S. Lives during COVID," *Scientific American*, June 13, 2022, scientificamerican.com.

42 Bad Faith, "The 'Woke' Approach to Racial Politics Is a Dead End. Here's What Democrats Should Do," YouTube, December 13, 2021.

43 Sean Illing, "How the Politics of Racial Resentment Is Killing White People," *Vox*, March 19, 2019, vox.com.

44 Daily Kos Staff, "Be Happy for Coal Miners Losing Their Health Insurance. They're Getting Exactly What They Voted For," Daily Kos, December 12, 2016, dailykos.com.

45 Paul Demko, "The Ballot Revolt to Bring Medicaid Expansion to Trump Country," *Politico*, October 19, 2018, politico.com.

46 4 News Now, "Reclaim Idaho Travels State to Promote Medicaid Expansion," YouTube, August 15, 2018.

47 Gabrielle Gurley, "Breaking the Ballot," *American Prospect*, January 30, 2024, prospect.org.

48 Cedric Johnson, "The Wages of Roediger: Why Three Decades of Whiteness Studies Has Not Produced the Left We Need," *nonsite.org*, September 9, 2019.

49 Kyle Strickland and Felicia Wong, "A New Paradigm for Justice and Democracy: Moving beyond the Twin Failures of Neoliberalism and Racial Liberalism," Roosevelt Institute, November 3, 2021, rooseveltinstitute.org.

50 Felicia Wong and Kyle Strickland, "Beyond Racial Liberalism," *Democracy*, November 16, 2021, democracyjournal.org.

51 Andrew Kohut, "From the Archives: 50 Years Ago; Mixed Views about Civil Rights but Support for Selma Demonstrators," Pew Research Center, January 16, 2020, pewresearch.org.

52 Juliana Menasce Horowitz, Kiley Hurst, and Dana Braga, "1. Views on the Black Lives Matter Movement," Pew Research Center, June 14, 2023, pewresearch.org.

53 Johnson, "The Wages of Roediger."

54 Jose A. Del Real, "Some White People Are Pouring Out Their Hearts—and Sending Money—to Their Black Acquaintances," *Washington Post*, June 6, 2020, washingtonpost.com.

55 Lena Dunham (@lenadunham), Instagram, June 4, 2020.

56 Tiffany Camhi, "Some White Oregon Homeowners Are Selling at a Loss to Black and Indigenous Buyers," *NPR*, May 18, 2023, npr.org.

Conclusion

1 Mark Dudzic, "What Happened to the Labor Party?," *Jacobin*, October 11, 2015, jacobin.com.